WHEN THE COWS LIE DOWN

WHEN THE COWS LIE DOWN

THE REASON PEOPLE QUIT YOU—THEIR "LEADER"

Building and Maintaining a
"Max Fab" Culture of Success

Dave Nordel, CMSgt, USAF [Ret.]

When the Cows Lie Down: The Reason People Quit YOU—Their "Leader"
Published by Max Fab Consulting
Billings, Montana, U.S.A.

Copyright ©2023, DAVE NORDEL. All rights reserved.

No part of this book may be reproduced in any form or by any mechanical means, including information storage and retrieval systems without permission in writing from the publisher/author, except by a reviewer who may quote passages in a review. All images, logos, quotes, and trademarks included in this book are subject to use according to trademark and copyright laws of the United States of America.

NORDEL, DAVE, Author
WHEN THE COWS LIE DOWN
DAVE NORDEL

Library of Congress Control Number: 2023913608

ISBN: 979-8-9880174-4-8 (paperback)
ISBN: 979-8-9880174-5-5 (paperback)
ISBN: 979-8-9880174-6-2 (hardcover)
ISBN: 979-8-9880174-7-9 (digital)

BUSINESS & ECONOMICS / Leadership
BIOGRAPHY & AUTOBIOGRAPHY / Military
PSYCHOLOGY / Mental Health

Editing & Cover Design: Chris O'Byrne (jetlaunch.net)
Interior Design & eBook: Michelle M. White (mmwbooks.com)
Publishing Management & Consulting: Susie Schaefer (finishthebookpublishing.com)

QUANTITY PURCHASES:
Schools, companies, professional groups, clubs, and other organizations may qualify for special terms when ordering quantities of this title. For information, email info@maxfabconsulting.com.

All rights reserved by DAVE NORDEL and MAX FAB CONSULTING.

This book is printed in the United States of America.

*To those of you who continue to inspire me
and help me make Giving Back a joy.
Also, to a very special person who gave me the words
to share about her husband, my dear friend who was my confidant.
Kim, this one is for Paul, who we all lost too early in life.
He will always be missed, and so many are
blessed to have had him in their lives!
My "Shirt" lives on forever!*

Contents

Prologue 1
Introduction 3
Save a Career, a Life, or a Relationship 3
First Sergeant (Shirt), a.k.a. Paul 5
Maximum Fabulous—Are You? 13
When the Cows Are Scared 17
You Don't Have to Lose Your Fingers to Learn 24
Orphans 30
The Line at the Coffee Bar 36
My Three-hour Cappuccino 40
I Will Never Wear a Watch Again 44
Godfrey 48
Uncle Stan 53
Don't Un-reward People 59
Quit Working 64

Leaders Pick Up Their Own Shit First 67

Quit Being a Tough Person 71

If You Want to Be a Leader, You Must First Have Followers. 75

Get Over Yourself—*Quit* Flexing in the Mirror 81

Does It Always Have to Be Your Idea? 87

Celebrate! Because If You Don't, That Genie Won't Go Back in the Bottle . . . 91

Nurses of Torrejon 96

Can a Medic Build a Bomb or Fix an Airplane? 103

Clear the Beds 110

Don't Lead by Hitting the Send Button 119

Leadership Starts with the Leader—
   Why Do Your People Leave You, the BOSS? 122

Quit Lowering the Bar 125

Navigating PTSD and Moral Injury 130

Overcoming Pain and Fear 132

Acknowledgments 137

About the Author 139

Prologue

This book is about quitting—is quitting good, or is it bad? It can be both. I can tell you that a restaurant owner sees nothing good about quitting. That moment when the manager walks off the job and leaves the store unopened—or worse—is about bad quitting, and the reasons need to be explored and corrected, if possible, because it affects the bottom line.

Then there is what you might call good quitting. You might compare it to the elite military special operations communities that *need* some people to quit. They try to get you to quit, and for the strength of the team, they need you to quit because they require a specific type of employee or a particular operator. This is a culling of the roughest kind, but it is necessary. I will cover both types of quitting and recognize that you may see quitting as good. However, today's question is why people are quietly quitting, leaving the workforce, not wanting to be part of an office environment, and quitting the social aspects of work as well. If you're going to explore good quitting or use the model I describe, then you can use the reasons I outline for why people are quitting their leaders to your advantage.

I also highly emphasize self-talk in these chapters, and discuss how we conduct these internal conversations to motivate us and help us work through pain, fear, stress, and the anxiety of challenges and conflict. The struggles that keep us from being who we want to be and getting where we want to go. The positive self-talk accompanying success is founded on a healthy self-image. This needs to be foundational to overall success for you—the leader. That is a mentality that you must constantly work on and understand.

These stories are meant to cover real situations where quitting is an option, and how you can avoid having your direct reports quit you as their leader and instead inspire them to press forward and thrive.

If we look closely at situations and stressors, we see that they may be simple, abstract, complex, or straightforward, but when it comes to you, the leader, it is simple. The new generation is values-centered; they not only read and observe your institutional values, but they also watch you for a consistent demonstration of those values. If those values are misaligned, your people leave—they leave your values, and they leave you. If you want a different outcome, please keep reading.

Introduction
Save a Career, a Life, or a Relationship

As I start on this next journey after being encouraged to continue sharing and giving back, I had to ask myself how I can continue from my first book, *Giving Back*, and shape my thoughts and experiences to encourage you to continue to be introspective and reflective. I found that when I talk with people and share my experiences, I hear a few common reactions. They usually consist of comments like "I never thought of that," or "I have had a similar experience and I need to pass that along," or "This really made me stop and think," or "Your story changed my life in a way that was positive." These comments are all inspiring and drive me to continue to share.

When we are open and vulnerable and share these moments in time, we find that the sharing helps others and even ourselves to make a positive change. We all continue to grow until our final day. I hope the "cows" in these stories make you better and help you answer some questions or overcome the struggles you may be experiencing.

If you research the word "quit," the first definitions you'll find are to give up, to admit defeat … but when reading further, you'll see the word described as "To set free, to make full payment, to depart from." Those are the words that resonate with me. Some do not give up or accept defeat. Some are set free after full payment and depart the battlefield, receiving a full reward.

This text will take you through a myriad of experiences tied to my key moments, travels, tragedies, and near-tragedies in my life, with my observations of the successful and not-so-successful approaches, behaviors, and routines that are healthy or unhealthy and need to be continued or changed.

We will travel through my feelings and emotions as I navigated my approaches to find organizational success when failure seemed inevitable and as I traveled the hills and valleys of personal challenges. I'll show you how you can be the catalyst of positivity or you can unintentionally destroy your status in an organization.

This book is about quitting, written by someone who was raised to believe that quitting was not only unacceptable but a sign of weakness. I was taught that you always keep going and run through the finish line in everything you do. I'll take you through the nuances of quitting, when you should quit, and how to quit and raise your game. I still believe you should work hard, run through finish lines, and complete what you have started, but there are times when you need to quit to succeed and quit to be healthy and quit to raise your game. There are also times when people quit their leaders. This is probably when the cows are lying down.

I hope you enjoy these stories and lessons learned as I continue to give back and share valuable data points to help you be a successful quitter.

Now let's get to quitting—enjoy the ride because it is all over the place!

First Sergeant (Shirt), a.k.a. Paul

A First Sergeant (Shirt) is the unit commander's personnel man or woman. They have a special position designation on their rank, and they hold a key advisor role in the structure. They assist, discipline, and solve all problems. For example, if your mom dies, you go see the Shirt; if your bills aren't paid, the Shirt finds you; and if the unit is marching, the Shirt leads the way. Shirts are not quitters by any standards. They work harder and longer than most; they sacrifice family and personal time for others, and rarely do they miss a formation or any work at all!

There is a reason this chapter is at the front of the book where it is best positioned to set the stage for the kind of *quitting* or *not quitting* we see and experience in life and leadership. I could not share this story without the help of my Shirt's dear wife, my friend Kim. She has guided me through her intimate moments with Paul and his demonstration of what we defined earlier as *quitting*—"To set free, to make full payment, to depart from." Those are the words that resonate with Kim, and she is the real author of this chapter. My words are merely additional thoughts on Paul's legacy. As Kim echoes about Paul, "Some do not give up or accept defeat. Some are set free after full payment and depart the battlefield and receive full reward." When it comes to Paul, I couldn't agree more! Kim's message in this chapter sets the stage for the book and for what is important in life.

We all have somebody close who faces extreme adversity. I have a few, and many of their stories could be in this book. One man stands out from them all—Paul, my First Sergeant.

I had many Shirts over my career. I had to see them from time to time for personal reasons, but this Shirt, my Shirt and my friend, was the poster child for all the things I describe. So why is this Shirt in a book about good *quitters* and *quitting* at all? Because when my Shirt wasn't given a choice to *quit* or not to *quit*, he navigated a journey we all must face—yet his was way too soon.

My Shirt was a kind man, a little taller than me, a person with a great sense of humor, and a wonderful dad and family man with a super wife, Kim. He was always there for me and all of us. I was a squadron superintendent, meaning we were together a lot while working on people and their wellbeing. Through this time, we became friends, leaned on each other, and helped each other through rough spots in our day-to-day lives.

At one point, I hit a rough patch in my career and I needed a Shirt. My Shirt took my call, and we worked through my problem; it was messy and required him to be the Shirt and not my friend. The story and its ending aren't as important as the fact that the Shirt didn't *quit* on me or my situation—not during or after, and we remained good friends.

My Shirt and I went different directions as we left our assignments for new ones, but we never lost touch. We communicated and shared constantly. Then one day, my Shirt called to tell me he was in a bad spot, he was worried, he had so much to do and so many to take care of, and he had a family that needed him. My Shirt had severe cancer. He was scared—not scared of dying but scared of *quitting*. He didn't want to *quit* his people, *quit* his family, and not answer the call.

In Kim's words, this was Paul's journey and his way of approaching the toughest of situations. We can all listen to and learn from him. Kim shares the following about Paul:

> I love to hear memories of Paul and how he impacted lives, and it is proof that his legacy continues to live on in the lives he touched. He is with me every day in my heart, and his love and legacy spur me on each day even eleven years after he left.
>
> I know this book is about quitting in different ways, and I struggle with the word "quit." I have pondered this and how Paul defined quitting. So, I share this with you all.
>
> I was blessed to walk through the valley of the shadow of death with my beloved for two and a half years. It was in no way a quick season. I watched as countless chemo drugs pulsed through his veins over the course of time and the horrific side effects of having the equivalent of a mustard bomb go off in his body time and time again. He never quit ... in fact, he became more determined and would put on his uniform and go to work just moments after being radiated or poisoned with a chemical cocktail.
>
> He defied all odds, and the medical team nicknamed him "Superman." Even after six weeks of being on a ventilator and in a coma, his strong heart refused to quit. I saw superhuman strength and was honored to stand beside him in the battle and be his voice when he could no longer speak.
>
> Even in a coma, he continued to touch lives. His motto, 'Attitude is Everything,' followed him each moment until Abba called him home. I believe those final moments of his life on earth were not ones he was deciding to quit but receiving further orders from the commander of his heart ... Abba was saying, 'Well done good and faithful servant, your

mission is complete, it is finished, the battle is won, and I am ordering you home.' Victory! He is healed; he is home.

He fought the good fight and finished the race. Eleven years after he was called home, I will continue to my dying breath to be his wingman, his voice, and live a life that reflects the love and legacy he shared with me.

I'd like to share a paper Paul wrote titled "Attitude is Everything." In the words of my "Shirt":

In the face of an adversity, attitude is everything
By Senior Master Sgt. Paul Y.

We have heard countless times during pregame and postgame interviews as athletes explain their strategy for the big win, "Attitude is everything."

It seems attitude plays an important role in success. I have told countless Airmen facing difficult situations the same thing. A positive attitude will play a major role in how things will turn out. You have a choice in how things will end up and how people around you will be affected. How you are perceived is 100 percent in your control.

I have used the "attitude" statement numerous times talking with Airmen and my own children. They were simple words, but how did they apply? Did those simple words, "Attitude is everything," really work?

In February 2009, I put those words to the test for myself. As I sat in the doctor's office on the edge of the exam table, waiting for what seemed to be an eternity, the doctor entered the room, and I could tell by the look on his face the news wasn't good.

The doctor took a deep breath and sighed when he said, "We reviewed the tests, and I'm sorry to tell you that you have cancer." I sat in disbelief as the feelings of shock, fear, anger, and denial ran through me. I didn't hear much of what the doctor said after that. My wife, who was sitting next to me, thankfully, was able to focus on the important information the doctor had for me.

Over the next few days, as I thought a number of things through, those words I had used so many times before popped into my head … "Attitude is everything."

I made up my mind at that point not to let the cancer get the best of me. I was not going to let cancer affect my family, my life, or my outlook on things. Anything less than a positive attitude would be unacceptable. I have tried to maintain as much of a normal life as possible with my work and family activities.

This past year has not been an easy road to travel. There have been many difficult periods, setbacks, and doubts on how things will turn out. With the support of my command, supervisors, family, friends, faith, and a positive attitude, this continuing journey has been more tolerable.

My father always told me, "Life is always easier when everything goes your way." Looking back, I think he was telling me to suck it up and deal with the situation in a nice way. So, with that said, how you approach situations is important and being positive can go a long way with you and those you work with, supervise, and influence. A positive attitude is an infectious thing and will catch on with everyone around you.

Always remember, especially when things are looking bad, "Attitude is everything."

A photo Kim took of the Shirt's shirt he wore for his chemo treatments.
He wore it every time they hooked him up to the caustic chemical cocktail.

This world gave the Shirt no choice but to *quit*; his cancer was advanced and aggressive, and he was on top of it with treatment, but he would be called home sooner than all of us wanted. What he did know was that there was a way to *quit*, to prepare himself for this eventuality, and to maintain his relationships and show his love. He kept himself dignified and honorable, all the while still trying to care for and feed those who needed it. My Shirt *quit* right, he was prepared, and he had plans, but mostly he gracefully left us in a manner that is my example of when given no choice (it may not always be death), there is a right way to *quit*.

The Shirt's strategy was to always have a positive approach, and he was infectious that way. I think of him often when my day isn't perfect. And I have certainly thought about him when it has been time to *quit*. No matter the reason—necessary or unavoidable—there is a way (the Shirt's way) to gracefully go and leave the lasting impression that you should.

The only thing missing here is to capture the impact that Paul had on everyone who he came in contact with. Paul always had an offhand joke and a way to make the difficult easy. He always put himself second in line when it came to his people, and he was "superman" in many ways. His heart was strong in more ways than physically. He was a once-in-a-lifetime friend and a follower of the Lord. I watched Paul do and say things that changed lives on the spot, and sometimes he championed solutions to problems and issues for others for months—he was a super Shirt and a super-human. This book would not be complete without paying him the respect he deserves and continuing to set him free after full payment to depart the battlefield and receive full reward. Godspeed, Shirt! You are the finest!

LESSONS FROM MY "SHIRT"

Think of a time you may have *quit* or stopped doing something. How did you do it and what was the lasting impression?

- The Shirt had given thought about how to *quit*; it paid off forever. He is the example.
- If you have to *quit*, keep your attitude in check; you may have to go back.
- Good *quitters* don't ruin relationships; they make them stronger as they go.

- Remember, you may not have a choice to *quit* and you may not have time to fix things, so keep your life in good repair—have a Max Fab exit.
- When you're faced with no choice but to *quit*, remember that "Attitude is everything"—the Shirt said so!

Maximum Fabulous—Are You?

In full disclosure, I am including this chapter from my first book for a variety of reasons. I have been on many speaking tours since I wrote the first book, and this message seems to be what resonates with people. I have promised you the key to Max Fab from the title of the book, and I'd like to add additional facts to the original story. So here it goes: one of my examples of a Max Fab success, and yes, I was watching to see if the cows were lying down and if a storm was coming—enjoy!

I've watched a lot of farmers over the years, both here in Montana and when I was young, talk about adversity, challenges, and what the future might hold. Sometimes the outlook sounded bleak or daunting. Things like dry weather or drought, disease creeping its way through a crop or a herd, or the price of grain or hay—it all can mount up and be crippling. The same is true in military operations: you can have long boring times away from family, you can have fabulous days, and you can get pretty down and lonely. The good news is there is a cure!

When I was rotating out of Iraq, the team threw together a quick go-away gathering for me. It was a bit more than I deserved, but one gesture stood out as a validation of at least one small thing I got right.

My daily routine consisted of a lot of push-ups (I hate push-ups) with the troops going off duty and coming on. It was my way to check on them, discover their needs, look them in the eye, and sometimes steal a phone from their hands to talk with their moms or dads (special teary-eyed talks, and so fulfilling). Regardless, we all did push-ups! By the time I was done, it was usually 120 to 150 push-ups, depending on who I ran into. As I did these buddy checks, I was asked, "Chief, how are you doing?" My response was always "Maximum Fabulous." This would inevitably invoke a curious smile and a "What is that?" question—I explained that this is the highest form of attitude you can have. You control that 100 percent, and it is where we all need to be to be successful, save lives, and go home sound in mind and body. The team before us was tremendous and had remarkable numbers, but our survival rates were almost 100 percent; if you made it to us alive, you stayed that way—organizational attitude saves lives!

There were a couple of items at the trauma center in Iraq that were unique. Some are now in the museums that surround our capitol in Washington, DC. One article is a large American flag (there were five or six total throughout the Iraq War) that was draped inside the small, covered tunnel known as Hero's Highway that led from the helicopter medical evac pad to the trauma bay. These flags were huge, and each of them has been preserved for history. We all would love to have one of those.

When my commander asked what I would like when I left, I said, "The medical red cross/red crescent flag that flew over the trauma center." He smiled and pointed out that those were hard to get. I knew this, but hey, you can ask, right?

Well, the day came, the going-away happened, and the commander sang karaoke (he is one of the finest leaders I have ever been around, but he is less of a singer). He shared some kind words that will never be far from my thoughts. He was amazing. When he stood up to speak, he presented me with the flag. It was a white flag that wasn't so white anymore. It was brownish from its time flying over our heads. Along the bottom of the flag, in bright red stitching, were these words: *maximum fabulous!*

To this day, that flag makes me think. It hangs where I can see it every day when I park in my garage, and it reminds me of the one thing I need to maintain every day: my attitude. Many aspects of life are outside of our control. As badly as we want things to be easier, better, or more of or less of, we can't control them. The one thing you can bring to bear each day is an attitude—a good, consistent attitude that is positive and breeds an infectious atmosphere within your close relationships and the people you lead.

Max Fab, as I shortened it to, became the rallying cry during tough times when we were lonely, tired, scared, or trying to deal with the difficult sights and sounds of a war zone trauma center. It was imperative that every day I brought my best: my best effort, my best physical and mental state, and my best attitude. I was like a virus; I was contagious, and I needed to control what I was spreading. I chose to spread *Max Fab*. It was the top of the food chain as far as attitude, and our team deserved nothing less.

I could have done a lot of things better during this time and throughout my career, but I know that when my attitude was *Max Fab*, it made everyone around me better, and that was what I could control all the time every day! The times *Max Fab* wasn't there bred the type of reactions you can imagine.

So make the choice, take it on, and challenge yourself. Present yourself as *Max Fab*, and change your family and the organizations that are lucky enough to have you! Those farmers I watched working so hard—they were *Max Fab*. They always had hope, and they were great role models.

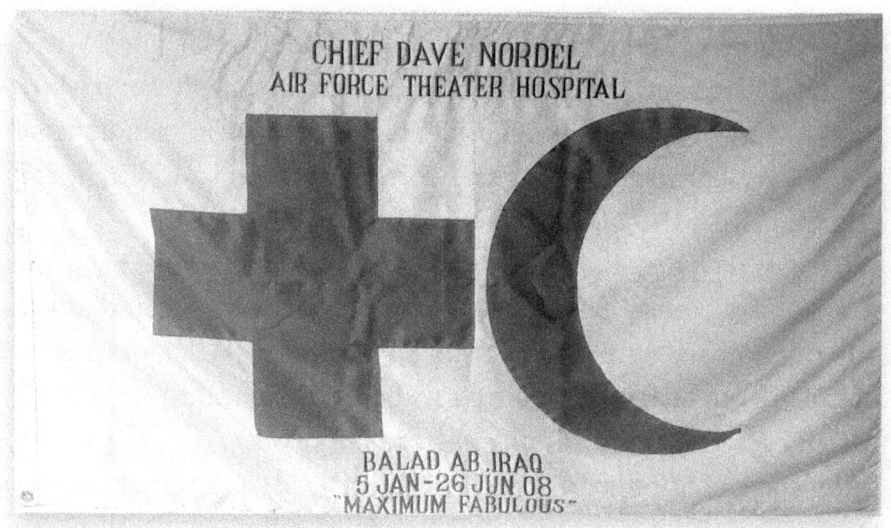

LESSONS ABOUT MAX FAB

How do you shape your attitude? How do you get to Max Fab?

- Shed the burden of worry about what you don't control.
- Transform energy into positive attitude development and control.
- Look for the opportunities in adversity; highlight them and make them *Max Fab*.
- Enthusiasm breeds enthusiasm.
- You own your attitude and how people perceive it. Be a good steward.

When the Cows Are Scared

We have much to learn from animals. One area I find amazing is that if you pay attention to their tendencies and habits and reactions, you can see and use the signs to predict future events in a way that can save money, time, and sometimes lives. For example, recently I was on a fishing boat. It was hot and humid, and the white billowy clouds of a Saskatchewan day were coming upon us. We were worried about the weather and threat of lightning, so we motored back to the dock to pull the boat out of the water and head to the house. It was precautionary, but we had a feeling the storm would come.

Then, like a jolt back to my childhood, as we turned for the boat ramp, we saw about forty head of cattle. They were all next to a tiny tree, and every one of them was lying down. The signs of danger were there. They subtly presented a key indicator for us to make the decision that would keep us out of danger and help us get out of the coming rain and away from disaster. These cows were literal signs. However, your cows are around you in your home and workspace, and sometimes they look like your followers.

When I saw the cows on the ground, I knew the meaning from experience, and I laughed out loud and said, "We better hurry up and get in the house, the cows are lying down." I have seen this many times, and rarely do the cows miss the forecast. If you look this up, some will say there is nothing to validate this phenomenon, yet others swear by it. I'll add this disclaimer: Understand that I have researched the research, and because of real-life experience, I choose to side with the cows (wry smile here). It is amazing and oddly reassuring as you see the signs, because it gives you time to prepare and look around. If you pay attention, you might not get hit by lightning—in a figurative and literal way.

As we navigate life and leadership, I share this example with people who need to be re-grounded in the basics. These are high-performing people who are good at what they do, but they are suddenly having some small (or big) challenges. The question I ask them is, "What are the cows doing, do you still check, do you notice the changes, or have you *quit* paying attention to the subtle (or not-so-subtle) signs of a pending storm, illness, or problem with our followers or processes?"

During my time in Iraq, we had some terrible incidents of suicide and near-death, self-inflicted injuries. I wish I could say this was infrequent, but the rate it happened was disproportionate and raised alarms. To me, it was the equivalent of getting caught in the storm or hit by lightning. What were the signs? How did they get missed? And what did we *quit* noticing or doing?

We have moments and times in life when situations become so normal that we don't give them their due justice. We either assume they will always be there (spouses included), or we take them for granted that in the event we have a need, we will always have access to help, assistance, or rescue. We think that if we dial 911, our problems will start to go away. Well, what if you drove by the fire station every day for thirty years, and you always saw a truck and firefighters, the flag was always flying, and the door was always open? But what if one day, a sign on the door said "closed"? Would you ask a question? Would you try and find out why? Would you ask who would show up if there was a fire or accident? We should never *quit* watching the signs around us and understanding what they mean. If they change, we must find out what the new normal is and if there is an abnormal that needs to be addressed. This may save a life, a business, or your relationship.

Let's roll the clock back to 2006, when I had just reached the highest rank achievable in the Air Force enlisted corps (Chief Master Sergeant). I was leaving Guam and heading to cold and blustery North Dakota. A follower of mine had recently told me he was going to quit the Air Force because he had the same assignment to North Dakota as I did. His reason was simple: he was a Black Airman, had interests and a lifestyle that weren't supported by the community there, and was worried about the culture in that part of the United States. These were difficult times for people from different cultures and value systems (see my chapter on this in my first book, *Giving Back! Life and Leadership from the Farm to the Combat Zone and Beyond*).

So why do I tell you this here? No matter what he said, what I heard this Airman telling me was that he was scared, uncomfortable, and losing commitment to our service and our nation based on what the institution was asking him to do. Was this one of those times when you say, "Do what the Air Force says or get out!" Or do you take the time to address the concerns? This Airman was one of my top performers, and I noticed signs of change in him. We discussed the possibility that we might end up there together, and through our discussions, I discovered that he loved to fish. There is a lot of fishing in North Dakota! We started there and saw this as a huge opportunity for his career with a new assignment.

The discussion helped him realize what was most valuable decision and outcome. I smile, knowing that my friend went to North Dakota, where he and his wife did very well. To this day, these two are still my friends, and they taught me a lot: they made me better. Noticing the "signs" of the times when people may leave you or, worse, take their lives, follows a similar dynamic. If you read my first book, you know I left home in 1984 with an empty toolbox when it came to navigating the diversity and cultures throughout our nation and the world. I had to work hard to understand people's challenges and concerns, and I had to change my vocabulary to start asking a lot of questions if I were to be a true leader. Leaders lose people when they are not leading, but in this case, we saved a great Airman... with a lot of help, mind you!

Sometimes the best people you have are the cows you should pay the most attention to. The message they send will probably save the entire group, but only if you take the signs and see the messages. I was blessed with a new Sergeant in my unit, and she came with a stellar record, numerous experiences, and a reputation as a good, young leader. We put her in charge of the area that takes care of our pilots. This is a big deal and needs to be done right all the time. She was doing great for a few months, but then the signs changed, her performance and attitude changed, and her commitment started to wane. She was getting ready to "leave"—to *quit*.

There was one supervisor between her and me on the organizational chart, so I had to let that individual work with her. Eventually, they came to me and said they thought she was a lost cause. We discussed what had been done, and thankfully, I had been mentored and taught that if you don't know, go find out. We scheduled a meeting, and when she arrived, she was definitely not the bright, shiny person who we loved to be around. She was sad and lethargic, and her body language said it all. I went through how accomplished she was, how she was doing so well, how much we were concerned, and that we wanted to help. Then the tears came—boy, did they come—and she started off with two things that were to be discovery learning for all of us. She was going to *quit* all of us. Her story went like this. "Chief, there is nothing here for me. I am uncomfortable in the community, and I don't fit in. My family is miserable, so we are going to leave the Air Force if you don't get me out of here." I asked for an example and knew I was in for one of the hardest parts of leadership—building empathy.

Her stories went like this: She explained how just last week, she was at the store. While she was waiting in line, she noticed she was the only Black person in the place. It wasn't long before she was approached by a lady who asked, "Are you from Chicago?" Ironically, she happened to be from Chicago, so she said, "Yes, I am. How did you know?" The reply was matter-of-fact: "I didn't know, but you must be from there because we don't get your kind in these parts." This racial comment was not a surprise to me because I had taken the time to learn about this type of situation from the people who experienced it. It did, however, gut me, and it was a call to action. I offered the idea that the lady was probably not a bad person but may be ignorant based on her circumstances. This opened up a brand-new discussion where I quickly realized that ignorance wasn't a good excuse for the interaction, and that we all can work to do better every day from whatever viewpoint we have! As we continued to discuss how to help with all the uncomfortable situations she was experiencing, I asked, "If I could change one thing for you, what would that be?" Her reply floored me. She said, "Chief, I can't even find someone to cut my hair." I was to find out that Black female hair takes a special touch. If I needed a haircut, all I had to do was go to the base barber shop, jump in a chair, get my high and tight, and go on with my day. I never realized how much getting a haircut could affect someone in a way that would change their whole motivation, and in some ways, start feelings of depression. This problem pleased me because I could actually help. I had two wonderful peers, both Chiefs, both female, and both Black. I didn't fully understand the problem, but I had built a network that I could draw from to help my Sergeant and solve at least one challenge. What happened next was magic. Once I put the three of them together, it started a sharing of experiences, places, and things that, although hard to find, existed. It opened doors for my Sergeant, it provided her with mentoring I couldn't provide, and best of all, she was back to the person I admired, and our team blossomed because of it.

Who is your Sergeant in life, work, and leadership? What have you done for them? What tools did you use to make something blossom? The subtle signs the cows show us are a gift so we don't miss what is important—are you missing anything right now that is important?

LESSONS FROM "LAZY" COWS

When have you missed the obvious signs, and what outcomes did you wish were different?

- Don't let the subtle things become so normal that you walk right by them.
- If the cows are acting funny—take a pause and ask a question or two.
- When your followers start lying down, you better check the weather report or the climate in your organization.
- Is your network strong enough to help you with situations where you may not be the best person to handle them?
- Simple actions like haircuts matter. Intervene and make the changes needed.
- People will leave you if they don't think you see them lying down.

- The cows lying down could be the last sign before a disaster in your life or someone else's, so take responsibility and act.
- After a suicide occurs, it is often said that the cows were lying down and we missed it

You Don't Have to Lose Your Fingers to Learn

When I was growing up in my small town of Orland, California, there were many lessons to be learned from the indigenous people, the locals, who had grown up there and made a living. Although the population was primarily Portuguese families, other immigrants lived there as well. The Johansen brothers were cornerstones in the community. They owned the local slaughterhouse and the butcher shop. Imagine an agricultural community that had beef cattle and dairy cattle. That's where everyone got their meat; if you sent a cow to the butcher, not only did they slaughter it for you, but they also made your hamburger and hamburger patties.

During my teenage years, I started to learn an important lesson that helped to shape my life. Sometimes you don't have to earn all the papers on the wall or complete all the fancy degree programs or similar formal trainings to make you an expert. Sometimes your diploma comes with scars or other visible marks. Those scars make others wonder what caused them, as in, "How did that guy get the scar on his face?"

Near the end of my junior year in high school, my mom took me down to the butcher shop, and we sat down with Xander Johansen, one of the owners. She said to him, "Hey, you know, the kid needs a job. You're looking for some summer help, and he could probably be your guy." I went in and was clueless about what I was getting into. I thought to myself, "Oh boy, what will I do? Why am I here? What do I know about butchering and meat?" But I politely answered questions. Xander stood up, shook my hand, and said, "I think, yeah, I think you can start Monday. Come on in, and I'll teach you the ropes." As I shook his hand, I noticed that he was missing his little finger and his ring finger on his right hand. I thought to myself, "Well, he's been a butcher his whole life; I probably have an understanding as to why he doesn't have those two fingers. But you know, there's always a story there."

Roll the clock forward, and I started working. I was still curious as to how he lost his fingers. My primary job was making hamburgers, and I made a lot of hamburgers and got to deliver them around town. I developed a knack for it and was pretty good. Not to mention, the job came with some benefits. All the girls I went to school with worked in restaurants that served burgers, and I got to do delivery and see the girls twice a week. There was a social aspect to the job, which was good since the job wasn't overly appealing. I guess you would call me somewhat lazy because I wasn't doing it up to their standards. After all, I was still trying to learn. Despite being new, people would ask, "Why can't you do this too?" or "Did you think about doing extra, going above and beyond?" I wasn't trying hard enough to excel, so I wasn't allowed to do certain things like use a knife to cut meat.

One day, they were boning meat to make hamburgers, and I had gotten ahead of the cutters. I was waiting for more meat to run through the grinder for more hamburgers, and one of them handed me a knife and said, "Hey, why don't you go ahead and start trimmin'? I am out of boneless meat." So, I was thirty seconds into boning meat out, and I heard this curdling scream. You know the type; it's accompanied by, "Stop! Stop, stop, stop what you're doing!" I had received some instructions on which way the knife needed to be pointed, and a brief rundown on how I should hold it safely. Lo and behold, I got a little irritated because I thought I was doing something right. I was following along and trying to listen, but then out comes the story about how Xander lost his fingers. He had lost those fingers a number of years back, and to keep a long story short, it came down to a lack of listening and attention to detail.

This story impacted me later when I went into the military, where people have a lot of ranks and are in charge of others. They're the leaders, and you look up to them. But sometimes the guy on the corner with a scar on his face is the person you want to talk to; he's the one to get your advice from. A scar can mean credentials.

We can pick up books and read them. Most of the time, when you read a book, you don't know the author. Many of us don't even spend the time to find out their credentials. Anybody can write a book; anybody can tell you anything. But it's nice to have the details backed up, and true credentials come from being able to back up those claims. Maybe there is a three-dimensional aspect of your life that you can use to back up your knowledge. Try using a story that is relevant to what you're teaching. Doing so will set you apart and position you as someone who knows what you're talking about—a good teacher.

For example, suppose you want to tell somebody the five methods of how to do a task. A strong starting point would be to say, "Here's how I came up with the five methods, because I first tried twenty-five different ones. These are the five that popped out of that: the ones where I found the most success." Often, however, we try to shortcut the process by putting it in a checklist format. So, there comes a time when you need to walk across the room and ask that guy with a scar on his face how he got it, especially if you feel that it's relevant to where you're at in your leadership journey or your physical and mental health journey.

People are always around who have scars—scars that come from going through the battle you are about to face. Those scars can be literal or figurative. No matter how they were acquired, they have a story behind them that can help you become better at what you do. If you take notice and learn from their scars, you grow and become better without having to bear the same scars yourself. These individuals have recovered from those scars, and most are eager to share their experience and knowledge and teach us how to recover from the scars or, better yet, avoid getting them in the first place.

I learned how to use a knife and work in a butcher shop without stabbing myself, cutting myself, or hurting myself in any other way. I didn't have to lose a finger or two because I leaned back on the man without the fingers; I talked to the guy with the scar on his face. To put it another way, let's say you want to ride bulls for a living, and there are two people you can talk to. One is a guy who has ridden bulls for twenty-five years; he's got a scar on his face. The other is a guy standing there with a book about how to ride bulls; he has, maybe, attempted to ride once. Which one would you trust to teach you the art of bull riding?

This concept applies to anything in life. As we move forward and look at the situations that we walk into, we must be aware that sometimes we don't slow down long enough to look around the room. We miss the idea of going over and asking somebody how they got to where they're at. We don't take into account their experience, and often, we disqualify them simply because they don't have a certain three or four letters behind their name. They lack the credentials to which we assign so much value. Those are all relevant; however, when it comes to developing as leaders or managers and growing ourselves and others personally and professionally, we need to surround ourselves with people with high levels of practical experience. In most situations, it starts with mentorship.

How many of us truly have a mentor? Some of us *say* we have mentors. But do we have true mentors? Do we have appointed mentors who understand where we are now, where we came from, and what we went through to get here? Do they recognize what you need from them? Do your mentors know how to respond when you call for them? Mentors aren't people who you see once a day or even once a week. Sometimes mentors are people you reach out to when you're in certain situations. That mentor who has missing fingers or a scar on their face—they have been there/done that, and they know how you can overcome the challenges you are facing. When you run certain ideas by them to get advice on moving forward, they get it.

So, I ask, how many of us specifically appoint mentors? Or do we just throw a big, wide net out there when we have issues and hope someone with the right experience comes along to save the day? Do we run to the bookstore and grab the first "elixir" off the shelf that tells you how to mix a "cocktail" that will fix your leadership skills, business dilemmas, relationship problems, or even mental health issues?

Books are good, and they help us to be reflective and to think through issues we are facing. Then, we can apply critical thought to those issues and discover which guidance is most helpful. However, nothing can replace the true experience of somebody who has walked the walk, pushed the buttons, rode the bull, or butchered the animals. Experience has taught them how to do that, and they can pass that on to you.

It seems to me that it's a missing piece for people. Most people need to slow down a bit in life and seek out others to add into the equation of their personal development.

I challenge you to take the time to walk across the room and talk to the man or woman with a "scar" on their face. Remind yourself why you would rather learn from the person with a scar versus gaining your own scars. Can you build relationships that help build you? Can you put your ego in check long enough to grow—to truly grow?

In farming, you sometimes have to add fertilizer. In your own life and journey, who is fertilizing you, and what fertilizer are you choosing? Is it healthy? Or is it fertilizer that you picked only because it's the best or the easiest? Often, that fertilizer doesn't cut into the fear and pain of getting true feedback and having to grow. Just like with weightlifting, with growth comes a little bit of pain. It's all good pain. There are a thousand reasons to not do something. And there are a lot of good reasons to do something. How does that compete? Which reason will you listen to?

LESSONS FROM LOSING FINGERS

- When in doubt, go find out.
- Mentors are necessary.
- Choose the right fertilizer.

Orphans

I have been blessed with some cheerleaders in my life (these will be further addressed in a following chapter), and as they have inspired me to write these crazy stories and share my views on life, many of them have said, "Don't forget about the orphans, Dave. People need to know about the orphans."

We all know the traditional definition of an orphan, and it can invoke some less-than-pleasant thoughts. If you haven't been around an orphanage or even a foster home, it would be hard to truly sympathize with what it's like to grow up without a parent. Well, I had a catbird seat to a wonderful story that involved my great-aunt, my grandfather, and his brothers when they all moved north of the California valley, where they eventually established themselves as dairy farmers.

My grandfather's oldest brother died young on the farm from heart disease, and he left a young widow. She was my great-aunt, and she stayed on the farm after her husband's death. Her son eventually took over the ranch and began to run it. She was my grandmother's best friend, and we would often stop in to visit. Her house was on the corner with the county K–8 school, and in my memory, everything—the fences, the house, and all the barns—were vivid white.

These visits were always fun for me because my aunt had made a decision after being widowed that she would raise foster children. These were usually kids my age (seven, eight, or nine) or older, and they came from broken homes or other foster situations where things hadn't gone well. Sometimes the situations were worse than most could imagine. My aunt seemed to handle all this with grace. Most of the kids thrived while with her, and many went on to do very well later in life. For me, this lesson was full of hot summer days (many of them pushing 110 degrees Fahrenheit), chasing animals, learning from others, and riding (or, more accurately, trying to ride) a unicycle or pogo stick! Good ice cream and popsicles were a must, and there were always homemade goodies. The smells of the visits bring back fond memories, especially of fresh bread, blooming flowers, and the ever-present odor of the dairy farm. Of course, we can't forget the hot rocks under our bare feet.

At the time I observed my aunt and the children in her care, it seemed like the story was always the same: someone in need got help, and then everything got better. I know that not all the kids had a great time or stellar ending, but what I do know is that once they came to my great-aunt, none of them was treated as a foster kid or orphan; they were treated like family. They were given respect and the time and effort necessary to excel if they chose to put in the work and to change.

Why do I share all this? Since I left home for a long military career and then transitioned back into civilian life, I've seen a lot of personal and organizational orphans. I will give you a few examples and share my thoughts about why my aunt was successful and why she was an exception in many ways. When you are in a role that requires leadership (like running a foster home), one constant is work—you have to put in the work. If you are not working for and with your followers, you should expect no effort greater than yours from them. In other words, don't expect them to work harder than you do. By the way, "no *orphans* allowed" has to be the norm. This is a rule I have used when in leadership roles, and I followed the principles I learned from my great-aunt and found them to be tried and true.

I had been dealing with orphans for years as I started up the ranks of the Air Force enlisted corps. These "orphans" were not always people; they could be objects, processes, programs, and policies. I hated them and often became their "foster parent." They were boring and sometimes not "sexy" in the big scheme of leadership and management (they don't get you noticed). Unfortunately, these orphans are usually important and affect people's lives in ways such as pay, promotions, and quality of life. They need attention and effort to facilitate a thriving environment. My aunt helped her kids to thrive, and I paid attention to how she did that and why she was great. It brings me to the moment when I started calling these boring, mundane projects "organizational orphans," but you can call your orphans what you like. We all have them, and I strive not to have many (or any) in my life. To do that takes work, persistence, and being okay with working behind the scenes.

When I was in my first job as a Chief Master Sergeant, the orphans became a constant in my life. The organization I was in had a major inspection coming up for accreditation and certification. These inspections were not secret, and we had learned from all the other inspections across the Air Force. We felt prepared, and we should have been prepared. One of the constant write-ups every facility received was regarding the care and maintenance of a portion of the medical record we used as people were deployed to overseas locations. This record compiled all the information into a six-part folder with a snapshot of all medical history and any important information that medics at the deployed location may need (sounds important, doesn't it?). Well, every Air Force inspection prior to ours had failed at the currency and accuracy of maintaining these records. I was charged with making our result *great*! As I talked to the expert, I quickly found out that this document, the core document for deploying all members to the combat zone, belonged to nobody and to everybody. After I was told for the second or third time that "I only do this part but not that part," I quickly realized that this process and document were an organizational orphan.

My aunt popped into my head as I wandered back to the commander's office. I told him, "I know what the problem is." He said, "What do you mean?" I replied, "Nobody owns the form, and nobody cares about it because nobody is accountable. Since there is no interest in taking care of it holistically, it is poorly cared for." We quickly decided on a course of action, and we prepared it like this: Assign an owner, set expectations for the care and feeding of this orphan, schedule follow-up checks with the owner (my aunt would have unannounced checks from the state), and make sure the owner had all the necessary resources and support.

The look on the new owner's face was priceless; they looked like we had given them a lemon to chew on, and they knew it wasn't sexy. We spent time explaining the larger ramifications of not only inspection failure but ultimately mission failure with our deployed Airmen if this orphan wasn't taken care of. This seemed to help focus them, and we gave them a pep talk and resources. Then the hard part started where persistent work was required.

What we quickly learned was that you can't be supportive and resourceful and not help do the work. The owner also needed to work hard to show their charges that they were committed until the very end. This process went on for months, required some weekend work, and took valuable life balance time away until it was completed. This may sound extreme, but the orphan had been neglected for so long that it needed maximum effort to achieve the results we needed. This team became like my aunt—persistent, dedicated, and loving (in an administrative kind of way)—and they all made sure nobody felt like an outcast or that they were less important because they were working on this unsexy problem. The team succeeded, and the inspection was a success. Their phones rang repeatedly from medical facilities across the world, asking how they achieved their high ratings. The answer was that we simply stopped treating it like an orphan.

We all have orphans, or potential orphans, in our lives. We can treat most of them like my aunt did and make them successful, wanted, and appreciated for their contributions to the bigger picture. A few examples are the small gestures in a relationship and the time you spend on them, or the areas of your life that are boring and mundane that can make your experiences overall better. We all know orphans when we see them because of the state of their care and their need for attention.

In business, or as an entrepreneur, it is interesting as I ventured through my after-military life to see smart and accomplished people create orphans while they thought they were doing great work for the masses in an organization. The most impactful of them all was during the COVID-19 pandemic. As humans, we love structure, and with structure comes hierarchy, and with hierarchy comes levels. During a couple of my COVID leadership experiences, I watched accomplished people cause quitting at all levels—orphans were created daily. This was because, as they were trying to navigate the constant changes going on in the world, they stopped including the masses in problem-solving. Once that happened, they created new processes, new procedures, and new organizational structures without assigning leaders or champions—they created orphans. Soon, the orphans started to cost money and weaken the bottom line, and those affected by all this quit. Worst of all, the cows were lying down everywhere.

I have used the simple lessons from my aunt when leading projects or disaster activities. I implement the one rule that has always helped: never create orphans. Always have an owner of every person, process, and policy. Check accountability and make sure it thrives and never becomes an orphan. We identify and call out orphans and build a plan to fix the reasons something or someone is an orphan. How? We do the work and persist. Don't quit on your orphans: raise your game and make them feel loved.

LESSONS FROM *ORPHANS*

- It's okay to do the not-so-sexy work—it may be as important as the sexy stuff.
- Don't create orphans because you don't want to do the work.
- Orphans need a leader who will work as hard as they will.
- My aunt treated all her children the same; they never felt like orphans or foster children.
- When establishing your objectives in life or work, don't allow orphans; assign ownership and follow up on your charges.
- Don't create orphans or let them become a part of your life or organization.
- Nourish all that is important, even when it is not glamorous.
- People quit leaders who allow orphans; they want accountability.

The Line at the Coffee Bar

There comes a time when we need to see other types of cows and maybe adjust—or even quit—certain rituals and habits.

The length of time that people stand in coffee lines can vary depending on a variety of factors, such as the time of day, the popularity of the coffee shop, and the number of people ahead of them in line. On average, however, it's common for people to wait in line between five to ten minutes to order and receive their coffee. However, during peak hours or at particularly busy coffee shops, it's not uncommon for people to wait longer, sometimes up to fifteen or twenty minutes or more. On average, people spend 6,500 minutes, or 108 hours, every year in coffee lines.

At times, a simple moment strikes you funny and it brings the situation into perspective on a larger scale. We have all been there. I find it amazing that normally when you ask someone, "How's it going?" or "What have you been up to?" you get a rundown of their daily or weekly schedule (from memory), sometimes with dates and times. When I ask that question, however, I truly want to know how someone is doing. It makes me curious as to why we need to show others how full our calendars are or how "busy" we are. We define our lives by how busy we can be. Why do we do this, and, more importantly, is it healthy?

How much time do you spend each day, week, or year standing in the coffee bar line or waiting in the drive-thru? How busy does that make you? Are you really *that* busy if you are spending so much time in these lines?

I remember those early mornings on the farm: the sound of the machines coming on to start the milking process, the constant "clink-clink" of the chains around the cows' necks as they worked their way to the barn, the soft click of the radio as it started to play a series of songs that would be repeated over and over (you never change the channel), and the chore of getting water for the coffee pot. Back then, the coffee was a must before you started the milking. When I was a small guy, I wasn't overly contributing, maybe I was even in the way, but if you got the water for the coffee pot, you might get to milk a cow or two … fun, right? If the coffee wasn't ready, we didn't start our chores for the day. It was an informal rule.

When I was helping out, there were usually three of us: Mel, Charlene, and Davey Baby (as they called me). It was our little line at the coffee shop. The best of all was you got your cup, went to the first cow to be milked, and squirted your cream right from the cow into the cup. It was heaven, and my mouth waters to this day remembering it! As busy as we all were on the farm—with a totally full calendar, so to speak—we had time for this coffee routine. However, once we got the coffee, it was time to work, and we didn't always finish our cups of coffee, or they were cold by the time we got back to them!

Not long ago, I was in an institution that worked 24/7 operations. Most people I know who worked there were successful in life and professionally trained and educated, but when I asked how they were, I heard, "OH MAN! I am sooooo busy!" Then their detailed monthly or annual calendar came out. I smiled and said, "Really? Well, look at the line at the coffee bar. Most people go through this ritual three or four times a day, spending twenty minutes every trip when you include conversation and catching up. Think about it. Potentially a full hour and a half out of your *busy busy* day!" Makes one think about what we tell ourselves, what we believe when we do that, and how it conditions us mentally and physically. Not to mention the health state we maintain because of it.

Roll the clock back to a time when I was *busy, busy*. So busy that I had a Saturday pile for all the work I had to do. In my mind, I was the busiest guy on the planet with the United States Air Force's future riding on my ability to put in eighty- or one-hundred-hour work weeks. I was always ahead; I was superman! I have come to realize as I reflect on this time of being soooo *busy* that I, ironically, can't remember a single thing I did on Saturday or after hours that couldn't have waited. At the time, it felt like it was the end of the world. It wasn't, and I could have (and should have) had better balance. The one and only activity I remember that was truly important was the efforts I put forth for my people and their evaluations and recognition. Everything else could have waited … and I could have spent time with my boys and my wife and worked on balancing myself!

One of the most compelling arguments for quitting certain habits is our mental health. People who do things well have the time and space to do them and also make time to recover so they end up mentally and physically healthier. Some of the Scandinavian countries have been changing to four-day work weeks, still with eight-hour days. They have minimal lunch and defined outcomes for those hours spent; I would argue they figured out the signs of the coffee line. The goal is to be productive, accomplish tasks needed for the "company," and then find balance. Take your time and be mentally free from the task at hand. This builds more committed and focused teams who stay with the company longer, are less of a drain on the insurance and lost-time bottom line, and are happier people who appreciate their balance. The result is all positive for the person and the company, so why not rethink the time we have on our calendars? Why not say, "I have a manageable day and it should be low stress." instead of looking to fill the white space in your life ... give it a try?

LESSONS FROM THE COFFEE LINE

- If you have white space, fill it with balance, not another meeting.
- Everyone is busy, so stop trying to be the busiest; it doesn't impress anyone.
- What will you do with the time you spend in the coffee line when you get it back?
- Remember to make the coffee early and grab a cup; the cows need to be milked.
- Coffee tastes better after all the chores are done; stop procrastinating.
- Respect other people's time; they may not want coffee.
- Stop trying to get to NO and try to get to YES.
- A working lunch is not lunch; it's work.
- All leadership starts with internal work.
- People quit leaders who don't offer balance or who demonstrate they are unbalanced.

My Three-hour Cappuccino

I bet you are thinking, "What is this all about?" or "I have never had a cappuccino," or "What's a cappuccino? I drink drip coffee," or better yet, "Thanks, now I want a cappuccino." I have been blessed to live in many countries and travel broadly, not only during my time in the Air Force but also on my own. I came to realize how fast we go as Americans. We grab all we can in the small amounts of time we dedicate to the chore, task, or event. We tailgate to prolong an event that is actually about two hours. We smash everything we enjoy into a morning and afternoon, and then we are off to the next event, fun activity, or work chore. It's a constant go-go-go, as we pride ourselves on being busy, as though busier means more successful. As I traveled and lived in countries like Turkey, Saudi Arabia, Spain, and the territory of Guam, I quickly learned that every place has its speed limit, and frankly, I see why some cultures have less stress and more happiness. We should all have both of those, and most of us strive to do so.

When I was deployed to Hungary, I was with some buddies, and we were exploring a local town. They wanted to go see everything that was in the tourist guide and cram it all into a small amount of time. I suggested we have a long lunch at an outdoor café. I told them, "You'll see more, learn more, and enjoy more." This was a boxing match of desires, and they all felt they needed to keep moving. I must have been persuasive enough because ultimately, they decided to try it my way. We found a nice, semi-quiet place at an outdoor café right next to the walkway and the street. We settled in, and our orders looked like this: beer, beer, beer, and a beer.

I said, "Let's have some finger food of a local variety," and out came the meats and cheeses and the simple foods that are incredibly tasty and indigenous to this part of Hungary. It was a big hit. I looked at the guys and said, "You never would have had this experience at a museum or on a tour bus!" The beers quickly disappeared, and we started on a second. I watched my buddies as they visibly relaxed, and that pressure to be moving and on the go dissolved away. They commented on a new smell; it was a rich scent of food. Unable to pinpoint this somehow familiar yet unfamiliar smell, we found a way to ask the wait staff what it was. We learned it was the local bread being made. You can guess what happened next: we wanted bread. The staff brought us bread made at the same place where we had smelled it. It was fresh, and so was the butter! I soon heard comments from my buddies like "This is the best!" and "What an awesome place!"

This part of Hungary had been occupied by the Russian military during the Cold War times, and the people reflect that in their looks. They are gorgeous people with dark skin and light eyes, they move around by walking or biking, and they are generally fit. This was not lost on my buddies, either... their approval of our choice to experience all of this by slowing down and watching and smelling and feeling was evident. What I saw was people truly relaxing. They were now in a state that was healthy as the pressure to perform, move, or gather up all they could in a minimum amount of time was gone. All they had to do was enjoy their three-hour cappuccino.

Have you ever driven over a hundred miles per hour? Most people probably have. When you drive that fast, you may say, "I just went from this point to this point." When someone asks if you saw the new farm or flock of geese or a break in the road, your response can only be, "No, we were going too fast. We wanted to get where we were going, and we were in a hurry."

When you grow up in a dairy farm atmosphere, the world moves quickly. If the sun is shining, there is work to be done and the to-do list never ends. In some ways, our lives are like that too; we plan vacations to get away from it all, then later say, "I need a vacation to recover from my vacation." You say you had a great time and saw so much, but did you? Did you recharge? Did you smell the bread or even know it was being made? Did you eat the finger food or notice the culture as it walked by?

I chatted with a cousin who has a similar life experience, and we laughed about the three-hour cappuccino. We both agreed that at those times, it feels good to be insignificant. You don't have to be noticed or busy or "productive"; you get to melt into the background, be a part of the stone or the wall, or just hold still like a plant in the corner. You can be so insignificant that you experience things you would never see, hear, feel, or taste if you were going too fast and being visible. Nature and culture happen naturally when you blend in, like being in camouflage. It is liberating, and you feel like you are in some way getting a bird's eye view of everyday lives you wouldn't normally see; they become your secrets and your bag of impressions, all while enjoying a cappuccino.

You may be thinking, "Okay, Dave, where are you taking me? What are you thinking?" Being insignificant is powerful. Watching, listening, hearing, smelling, and taking the time to do it all is powerful. There is power in understanding and appreciating differences and learning about activities that enhance our health and balance. It makes you change in positive ways and opens your ability to consider and understand other people and cultures rather than hold on to old viewpoints that they are different and, therefore, weird. Slow down and smell the bread. Sip the cappuccino. Try insignificance, and you might find it adds to you in a way that opens your aperture in life and culture.

LESSONS ABOUT CAPPUCCINO

- Walking outside an airport doesn't mean you have been to that place—not until you have a cappuccino.
- If something smells fishy or different, don't dismiss it as weird. It might be fresh bread.
- Relax and learn to absorb what is around you; what you absorb makes you grow.
- Grow by going slow.
- Slow days are not lost days.

I Will Never Wear a Watch Again

I find a watch to be an amazing device, as the grip that time has on each of us is enormous. Looking at our watch, and now cell phone, to see the time actually changes our vital signs—our heart rate rises when we feel we may be late. We change from one point of attention and quickly to the next based on what time it is and what is scheduled next in our lives. Even reading this may make you anxious as you begin thinking about being without your phone or watch.

To a farm kid, a watch is an odd thing. Yes, you need it, kind of, but it can also get caught in machinery and badly hurt you. It usually gets broken quickly, so having an expensive watch was exclusively for going out and formal occasions. The watch on the farm is less important than in other places. You know the cows need milking around 4 a.m., and if you start at 4:15, that is okay. You really only need the watch when you have to stop working to get to church or another function. As the watch entered my life in an environment that was totally reliant on it, I found a great opportunity to *quit* the watch at one point, and so I did.

When I joined the military in 1984, there were no cell phones or fax machines, and certainly no computers. The most technical item in my life was my watch. Like almost everyone, I learned to tell time in school. I had those papers I would take home to write the time under the picture based on where the hands were on the clock. Today, surveys show that 16 percent of people can't tell time on a clock with hands on it. In fact, I argue they don't even care because their phone does it for them. The watch of today is a feature of a phone and computer, and the traditional watch is a thing of the past.

The watch has been replaced, but the time it tells and the physical response to time remain unchanged. I remember early in my career when it was time for a time hack where we synchronized our watches with the time on the central command clock or the leader's watch. Once that was done, everything was coordinated off that time: when to go, when to stop, when to move, and when to drop bombs or attack. It was all set by the clock. I lived with my watch and couldn't operate without one. Being a medic and a nurse, you need it to take a pulse and check for respiratory rates. Over time, I grew to dislike my watch and the physical changes in my heart rate and anxiety level that a small glance at it would send through me.

I retired in 2014, and the first thing I did was lose the watch. Don't get me wrong, I have my phone to tell me the time, and I still have to be at certain places, but I took the reminder off my wrist. I removed the distraction, and it has helped me focus on what and who is in front of me instead of the next responsibility according to the clock. My heart rate doesn't jump, and I don't operate at a heightened sense that makes me unhealthy and drains my energy.

This isn't just my experience, either. Research shows that when people look at the time or at their watch, it can cause a sudden jump in their heart rate due to a phenomenon called "anticipatory response." The act of checking the time often triggers a subconscious reaction in the body, where the brain starts to prepare the body for whatever task or event is coming up next.

For example, if someone checks the time and realizes they are running late for an important meeting, their body may release stress hormones like adrenaline and cortisol in response to the perceived threat. This can cause a temporary increase in their heart rate and blood pressure, plus other physiological changes as the body gears up for the upcoming stressor.

Similarly, if someone checks the time and sees that they have a few more minutes before their next task or appointment, they may experience a sense of relief or relaxation, which can cause a decrease in heart rate along with other physiological changes.

Overall, the body's anticipatory response to checking the time is a natural reaction to the perceived demands of the environment and can vary depending on the individual's emotional state and expectations.

I made rules for myself, such as that I don't schedule events back-to-back because I don't want to place a time stress on myself. I am better organized and more punctual because of this breathing space in my schedule. I *quit* my watch, changed my method of time management, and developed a balanced approach to my schedule. Because of this decision, I raised my game and improved who I am, and this continues to play out in many other aspects of my life based on people, places, and experiences.

The watch was a *quit* that I am proud of. You can replace the watch with whatever causes your heart rate to rise, your breathing to change, and a feeling of anxiety to come over you in response to the hands on a clock or the ding from a cell phone or computer calendar reminder. It's okay to quit these stressors and improve your game by eliminating or reducing your reliance on whatever your "watch" is in your life.

LESSONS FROM QUITTING THE WATCH

What are the figurative "watches" in your life? What is stressing you out, and what can you do to better manage that?

- If something or someone makes your heart rate jump in a negative way, quit it or change your game.
- Time management belongs to you, so make it a healthy endeavor, and you will live longer.
- Just because everyone else is wearing a watch doesn't mean you have to.
- Do what works for you, not what everyone else is doing.
- Listen to what your body tells you when you look at your watch; it is real.
- Don't be the cause of what makes you anxious or short of breath.

Godfrey

When I was a young guy, I was fortunate when it came to having what I needed—I didn't get everything I wanted, but I usually got the things I needed. I also had family members and buddies around, and for the most part, life was steady and predictable. Everyone experiences levels of hardship, and we all travel through challenges. Humanity is connected and people experience life similarly and face many of the same troubles. For example, a person in Australia will have similar challenges to a person in the Congo, but what differentiates them is the extraordinary means that one must go through to deal with a life challenge based on the place they occupy.

My mother and I worked on our challenges together, and when it is just two of you against all that the world brings, you develop a relationship of survival and a focus on the basics. We had to work together on tasks we enjoyed and others that were not much fun. Sometimes we had to figure out how to make the bills work, and other times it was finding a way to have a little extra to enjoy. As a young boy, there were times when my summer job money went to help with the bills (see the chapter on sheets). I didn't fully understand how these times in my life were that significant—not until I met Godfrey. I will use his name here because this honorable man, a true giver who was always moving forward, had a smile on his face and may be one of the most influential leaders I have ever met in my entire career and life.

I had been to many places before I met Godfrey; I sat and listened for hours to the laborers in countries around the world tell me why they left their families—sometimes for multiple years—to take jobs so they could provide for their families. I was always moved emotionally, and it made me feel small among these people who gave so much to make sure those they loved had everything they needed.

One decision set Godfrey aside from all the others; not only was he far away from his wife and kids in Uganda, but he was also in a combat zone in a conflict that was not related to his country. He was guarding people he did not know and all the while charged with leading more than thirty men in this task.

When I arrived at the trauma center in Iraq as the Chief Enlisted Manager for the facility, I was promptly given the obligatory walking tour filled with handshakes, quick intros, and the "How ya doing?" stuff that goes on during the first day at work. This day was different because I was meeting people who had already had their lives changed by this conflict; they were dedicated and hardened, and most were honored to be there. I was just the new guy (Chief or not), and they were all feeling me out.

As we went to the helicopter pad so I could see the routine for casualty care, I was met by a stunning character. He stood six feet tall, had dark black skin, was dressed in brown utilities, and he had an automatic weapon with him—one I recognized as foreign and was less familiar with. As I put my hand out, I was greeted with a million-dollar smile by the most genuine of people. I shook his hand and said, "I am Dave. Nice to meet you." The stunning chap said, "I am Godfrey." This simple exchange started a relationship of a lifetime.

Godfrey quickly made sure I was knowledgeable on the roles each of them played in our security detail and how they helped with casualty care. Godfrey was the boss. He knew it, and his men knew it. I knew I needed him on my side if I was going to adequately take on the challenge in front of me! My blessing was that Godfrey spoke excellent English, and so did most of his men. I remember thinking, "These guys control every door, every passage, and they have to get it right, or we could have a tragedy. Are these people willing to die for me on a bad day? Or are they just drawing a paycheck?"

Godfrey's team was made up of Ugandan men working for an international security company, and they were hired to protect our medical resources in the combat zone. Their duties included basic perimeter security, and they had a man at every door, checking everything that moved. But their most important job was making sure that the wounded (enemy and friendly) did not get into the trauma areas with weapons or booby traps. They were the last line of defense for making us safe, and they took it seriously. I was a little out of my element there. I knew what motivated my Airmen and Soldiers, and perhaps a Sailor or Marine at times, but I didn't know why they were here. Why would they put it all on the line for me, and the rest of us, and why should they help care for friend and foe so professionally? Thank goodness I was blessed with Godfrey.

Over the following days and weeks, I got to know Godfrey better. As we got closer, I asked a lot of questions about him and his men, and I started to better understand each of them. What became obvious was that they were all doing this work to help and support their families. Godfrey ended up being the provider of some key lessons that never would have been mine to absorb had he not led and taught me. Godfrey explained to me that he had been away from home for years. He had a handful of small visits back, but for his family to survive and prosper, it required him to take on this kind of work. He was motivated by the ones he loved, and that allowed him to give much to us and his men. He was taking care of thirty families, as I would put it. He took care of his men so he could take care of their families and his family at the same time. His motivations were pure, real, unselfish, and grounded in values that some may never possess.

While I was there, I noticed that our guards and facility staff didn't have any recognition for special achievements, and in a place like this, a lot of that was going on. I asked Godfrey to help me do that for his men and to tell me what was appropriate (you just can't throw them a twenty-dollar bill). Godfrey thought I was crazy; he said they were just happy to be there, grateful for what they had and the opportunity to support their families. However, together, we decided to make their lives even better! Godfrey retaught me some lessons I had forgotten, and he taught me some new ideas about how to live an honorable life. He taught me about what is important and how moving forward and giving back can all happen at once.

One of the greatest compliments I have ever received was when Godfrey introduced me by saying, "This is my Chief." Together, we formed a bond and grew with each other to a point where our respect and admiration were possessive of each other. Godfrey is still in my life today, although mainly on Facebook and in short notes. He is a man of honor and a person to emulate. I was, and still am, blessed to have him in my life. He grew me through his example and gave me a perspective about what is true giving and true selflessness. Thank you, Godfrey, my dear friend and protector.

Godfrey can always say that nobody quit him, and he was always raising people up and making them feel special. He was a leader; he always saw the cows lying down, and he never had an orphan in his midst. He was under-resourced and faced challenges most of us never will, yet he outperformed many of the developed leaders I have known. He has never stopped giving of himself, and the results are an example for anyone anywhere.

LESSONS FROM GODFREY

- What is important to you? Make sure you really know; you only have so much time and energy.
- You show strength and are more enriched by generosity, respect, and selflessness than by money and status.
- Take care of many if you can; it makes the herd healthier and happier.
- You probably don't have it so bad; it takes a Godfrey in your life to keep you grounded.
- Be thankful for the abilities you have and be proud of who and what you are!
- Are you as dedicated as Godfrey was to his family, his men, and to us? Can you be?
- Don't lose touch with your Godfrey; the gift keeps coming, and you can keep giving!
- Grow while growing others; it is the best!

Uncle Stan

When you are a young person, you have so much going on that shapes you: good and bad experiences, huge wins and terrible mistakes. We have experiences we wish we could relive and regrets we wish we could erase from our memories and never bring up again. Regardless, these all shape us.

As I have shared before, my father left when I was around two years old; he was never a part of my life after that. I did have some brief encounters, some of which I will share, but basically, he quit on my mom and he quit on me. My father was a quitter. He decided to really quit, to walk away and not raise his game. This is one of those life events that shape you. I had plenty of male influences in my life and piles of cousins who felt like siblings at times, but I didn't have a father. This wasn't my fault, but it surely had a price.

I will stay true to the title of this book and to my belief that there is a time and a situation when quitting is "okay," but it is about how you quit and recover and not about giving yourself permission to be a quitter. Remember my Shirt's example of a noble way to quit. My father chose a different way.

As a young boy, I had lots of love from my grandmother and grandfather, and my mom was always there as best she could be, and we found ways to have fun. I had older cousins who taught me to hunt and to fill some of those "dad voids." I didn't miss out on all the experiences a father brings, but none of them are, or were, my "dad." My father was a quitter who didn't raise his game. He lived a life of lies and left a mess when he passed on.

In 1968, the year my father quit on us, the world was void of cell phones, cheap airfare, and the ability to order online. My world was only as big as the places where I could walk or ride my bike. I couldn't Google search, and this made it impossible to find my father—or even try and find him.

When our two boys were born, in 1993 and 1995, I started to wonder what my father would think of them, how he would react to who I was becoming, and who the boys looked like. I was working a job where we got our first internet access over a dial-up connection, and it fascinated me! So, we bought our first computer. This was a Gateway Pentium 200. It came in a box that looked like a cow and was the top-of-the-line home computer at the time.

The computer opened the world of searching and research. I could now access the formerly inaccessible. This computer would help me find the whereabouts of my father—as I saw it, a second chance. Who knows what would be different twenty-seven years later? Maybe my father had raised his game; maybe he could become a good quitter. I was able to locate him in Arkansas; our last name is rare, and the names all matched up on a simple people search. This computer provided a number and an address; now all I had to do was pick up the phone. I had an opportunity to reach out, and my father had an opportunity to "unquit." I paused for a few days and talked to my mother, my uncle, and my grandmother, who all knew him long before me. I told them I had his info and asked what they thought. What I got from all of them was the same feedback: Don't get your hopes up, he will barely ask a word about you, and he will spend thirty minutes talking about himself if he stays on the phone at all. The feedback didn't make me want to run to the phone, but what the heck, maybe my father had raised his game.

I told my wife I would make the call, and I set aside a time without distraction. I was absolutely miserable and nervous, and my stomach told me not to do this. I was so fearful to find out if he was who he was portrayed to me, and that was a heavy moment in my soul and my heart. I wanted to give the man as much time as he needed.

When I called, his wife at the time, who was maybe his fourth or fifth wife, answered the phone. I asked if he was there, and she said he was out but would return that afternoon. I called back later in the day, and he answered. I asked if this was him by using his full name, and he said, "Well, who the hell is this?" I said, "This is your son." The rest was a blur, but it went more or less like this: He asked, "How tall are you? What are you doing in life? Did your mom remarry?" Then he said "Not bad" about my height, and he was surprised about my mom. He then launched into a twenty- to thirty-minute diatribe about himself and all the wonderful things he had accomplished in life. This included a lengthy military career, one that happened to be more successful than mine at that time, and how he was running the world in his Arkansas town. It played out exactly like my mother and uncle had said, and it fell in line with what my grandmother told me to expect emotionally. It was a wash; my father the quitter was a bad quitter. He had not raised his game. After all these years shirking his role as a father, he was teaching me about responsibility and how to quit when you had to quit.

Roll the clock forward thirty-five years from when my father left and seven or eight years after that phone conversation. I had been in the Air Force for nineteen years now, stationed in Japan and in a great job doing inspections and exercises. I was busy and working long hours, but this job had my information on that computer that had opened the world for all of us. I arrived at work early, as always, and after getting settled, I scanned my emails. In the batch of standard daily stuff was an email from someone I didn't recognize. The subject line merely read, "Same last name." I was going through my routine, so I opened it to scan it. What was in this email would change my life and teach me about good quitters and how they raise their game. This email outlined the life of a man who had served in the Navy, gone to college, had a couple of boys, and enjoyed a hugely successful corporate career. He outlined that he grew up in San Francisco, went to school in San Diego, and lived in Arizona. I was confused but quickly figured, "I have a rare last name, and it is natural to reach out these days." This was a poor man's DNA search. I wrote back and told him about me and that the last name was my father's. My father also grew up in San Francisco, but I have had no contact with him (I didn't mention the phone call). The reply email was a game-changer.

The follow-up email opened with, "Well, your father is my brother, and I haven't talked with him in years." This man went on to tell me about his hobbies and his family. I was obviously shocked, skeptical, and curious. I had always wanted a good medical history from that side of my family. So, I decided to start on that track. I asked about my grandparents and their lives and health as well as my newly discovered kin. We had a detailed back-and-forth and decided to get on the phone. I couldn't believe it. I had found my Uncle Stan, or rather, he had found me. He knew my story and about my mother, and he, in his unbelievable way, had not quit on me.

When Uncle Stan and I chatted on the phone, I learned that he loved many of the same activities I did and his boys were similar to me in many ways. We decided to stay in touch and keep sharing our stories. Uncle Stan also started to slowly let me know about my father. The information he had turned out to be life-changing.

As my father quit, Uncle Stan raised his game—not just for me but for others.

I was finishing one of my degrees at the time, and I needed to fly back to the States to complete a clinical course. I worked the trip so I could attend a conference in Las Vegas and do my clinical studies in Phoenix, Arizona. I made sure to carve out some vacation time and called Uncle Stan. We decided I would come stay a couple days with him to meet his wife and have time to go through the life and times of my new uncle, my father's childhood, and beyond. I felt comfortable in this as we had spent time covering much of the past and present. So off I went from Japan to Las Vegas. I rented a car and drove to Phoenix to complete my degree clinicals, and then I took time off to go see my new uncle. As you can imagine, I was nervous and excited all at once. My arrival experience was wonderful, and we jumped into good conversations.

Over the next couple of days, we shot some skeet, shopped together, and looked at photos. I got fully caught up on the family medical history and, of course, the life and times of my father as a child through my uncle's eyes. I wasn't too surprised to find he had problems with his mother, although I was a bit shocked to hear about his bad temper and the fact that he was a fighter. I was mostly shocked by this kind man who was healing some of my wounds and being such a giver of his time and memory. I had found a gold mine of precious resources for my heart and soul. Uncle Stan had never quit on me; he knew I was out there, and he found me, he raised his game, and he took on my father's big quit in life and helped me raise my game.

As I was getting ready to leave on my last night with Uncle Stan, he said, "I have one more thing to let you know. You have a sister (half sister); she is older than you, and we have stayed in touch for many years. She lives in San Diego, has a son, and has been married for some time." He offered to let me call her while I was there and to open another window in my life.

Uncle Stan was full of surprises and still is today. So, I called this lady. We chatted briefly and decided we should meet ... so off I went from Uncle Stan to my sister Margie. My sister—wow—never had one of those ... and she gets a whole chapter to herself in this book about quitting. She is not a quitter but rather a gem in my life. As for Uncle Stan, we have hunted together, and we stay in touch frequently. He recently let me know that my father had died from kidney and bone cancer and filled me in on what his life looked like at the end. That part of this story is for another time; I am thankful to Uncle Stan for all he has done for me. He has done more for me on a mental health and personal level than any uncle, aunt, or extended family member. He is goodness and always has my love.

LESSONS FROM UNCLE STAN

- When you quit, there is a right way to do it while raising your game.
- When an "Uncle Stan" comes into your life, don't run away; it is a treasure.
- When you quit, it can affect events and people that you don't even realize, so make sure you fully understand the effect of the domino you are pushing over and what collateral damage might happen.
- Don't let a quitter ruin your ability to raise your game; Uncle Stan didn't.
- Pick up the phone and make the call, answer the email, and be open to a trip into the scary unknown—you might get a couple of new cousins, an uncle, and a sister ...
- Never quit on ultimate responsibilities and the ones you love.

Don't Un-reward People

We all have different motivations, and not everyone gets excited by the same things when it comes to rewards. You may not get it exactly right with everyone when you reward them, but you can get close.

My wife once went to Africa before we were married. We knew each other at the time, and she shared with me that she had a choice of trips to take: one was a safari, and the other was to climb Mount Kilimanjaro. She asked me what I thought, and I told her, "You may get one chance to climb a mountain, but have fun whatever you do." One would think that if you didn't want to climb a mountain or you had no desire to see an African animal, the choice would be easy. For my dear wife, it came to one reward: if you climb the mountain, they give you a certificate. My wife was pumped up to climb a mountain, and she was super focused. The tour guides had figured her out: give a certificate, and she would climb the mountain. I'll take a guess and say that not everyone who climbs to above nineteen thousand feet in the air does so to get a certificate, but that certainly was my dear wife's motivation.

One of my prized possessions when I was young was a simple pin I got for making the first all-star team in baseball. That pin is still on my first hat, and it makes me smile. It was a tremendous reward yet very simple. As we gain responsibility for people and the directions in which we take them, we have to reward and motivate them. When times are good and everything is rolling along well, rewards are quite easy; they just show up. These rewards look like raises, extra vacation time, and sometimes even a certificate or a plaque! Another of my prized possessions is a small hot plate with a Care Bear on it. It was my first reward in the United States Air Force, and it was given by my immediate supervisors and peers. It still motivates me today.

As we get more experience, more responsibility, and, yes, older, we need to know who and what we lead. We need to know what kinds of rewards motivate, and we need to fully understand what demotivates or un-rewards people.

We have used un-rewards our whole lives; remember when you screwed up at school and got detention? That was an un-reward, just like being grounded or losing your phone or other privileges. This was done to teach a lesson. In our leadership and life, we need to get this right. Discipline is necessary and, yes, a good thing, but as you go through the process, the event cannot seem to your people that they have lost something; don't un-reward—give gifts or opportunities for growth. Missing this cow lying down will surely drive people to quit.

When I became a supervisor for the first time, I was bound and determined to be the best and get it right. I was going to accomplish every task, be there for my "troops," motivate them, and build the future. When all this was unfolding, the Air Force was changing its evaluation system. We had a cumbersome one-through-ten rating system that needed clarity and to not be diluted by ratings that showed no difference between mediocrity and excellence. So, we changed it. We went to a one-through-five rating and were coached on what "above average" and "excellence" meant (the difference between a four or five rating). We were challenged to help deflate a system that rarely gave the top rating.

We had some very senior executives and leaders traveling around, giving us the why and the how! I was new to these systems and had my two brand-new Airmen to lead. I was determined to be the perfect supervisor and the best boss, and execute all I heard exactly as I was told to! My two new Airmen were great young people who were both married, hard workers, and aspiring to be their best. I did everything right, conducted initial feedback, set expectations, and followed up with them regularly and as often as possible. They were a great pair and contributed to our unit well. Then I began to un-reward them. I started to take their hard work for granted, and I gave feedback as if they were perfect. I was happy they didn't cause me problems or need any discipline issues. They were both excellent! I should have taken the time to reward the simple things daily and say thank you at least once a week. But the one reward I missed was the tough feedback they needed and the method I was using to evaluate them.

To set the stage here, not everyone was as gung-ho as I was with this new evaluation system. It was easier to just give a five and move on. The five was non-confrontational, and it kept people happy. It was often a reward that wasn't deserved, and it was tied to promotions. We had lazy supervisors, and they started to inflate the system that was built to do the opposite.

But back to my two fabulous Airmen, who didn't know what was going on outside of their control, and I failed to tell them. My reward to them should have looked like this: "You are doing great in these areas, and you need to improve in these areas. If I had to rate you today, I would give you a (fill in the number here) and here's why…" I didn't do that. I was happy I had good Airmen not causing problems and figured they were happy! The lesson I learned from this mistake was painful.

The day came to officially write the reports about their glowing lines of accomplishments. The words to describe them had to match the number they received. This was their moment to be rewarded for all they had done! So, I did it. I did my part. I deflated the system (because the system told me to), and I gave them a good rating that was above average. I gave each of them a four. They were above average and good Airmen—congrats to them both! This was the ultimate reward of all.

However, these Airmen had friends—others doing similar work, Airmen who competed directly with them for awards and promotion—and guess what they all got on their evals? My four rating had just set them back. It was an un-reward and not balanced. Because I failed to communicate properly with them throughout the process, it was a surprise (and nobody should be surprised by this type of thing). The result was that two fine people who would have made great career Airmen quit to up their game. They left to join another organization that better valued their efforts; they quit to find a *good* boss. I had un-rewarded these two, and they left me. They *quit* their boss and then *quit* the United States Air Force. I got exactly what I had rewarded or un-rewarded. I missed the little things. I didn't stay informed on the bigger-picture stuff, and I took them for granted. So, they *quit* and took their game elsewhere.

LESSONS ABOUT UN-REWARDS

- The smallest rewards are the most important, so make sure you give them.
- Don't take good or great for granted. Nurture it, or it will change or leave.
- Change is inevitable, so don't let it drive bad decisions. Do your homework.
- Feedback is hard. It takes courage, and it is a gift to give and take.

- Bad leaders create quitters. If people you manage are quitting, run to the mirror.
- Remember those all-star pins in life and start handing them out—it matters!
- If it takes climbing a mountain in life to get your reward, go do it!

Quit Working

In my first book about chasing white space on your calendar and then stressing over it, I recommended that you fill it with activities other than work to remain healthy. I once listened to a senior leader who told me to quit working. He explained that you make more money that way. I asked him what he meant and to clarify how you make money by quitting. His response was refreshing and seemed a bit silly at the same time. He said, "You have to *quit* everything a couple times a day to be more productive." He went on to suggest that you stop your routine, close your eyes, and just think; think about anything that needs contemplation, and focus just on that. Once you have done this for ten or fifteen minutes, write a few notes, then go back to what you were doing. This made more sense to me than most other pieces of advice about productivity, and to this day, I still do it.

An emergency manager is always in preparedness and response planning modes and always playing the "what if" game. One of the first topics we discuss is how to handle the initial response to an emergency. The answer begins with step back, take a deep breath, and think. Make time to build a small plan. This applies to all situations, whether you are lost in the woods or have just been involved in a car accident. You *quit* doing and start thinking. These actions have saved many lives and may save your proverbial life one day too. The point is that stopping to think helps us refocus, clear our minds, keeps us mentally healthy, and gives us positive, good self-talk that can make us better and keep us from making rash decisions or mistakes under pressure.

I recently spoke to a large group of young managers who were working on becoming better leaders. Whenever I go into any leadership training, I emphasize being careful what you tell yourself because you are listening. Whatever you say should be positive and good. What I asked them to do was reflect on aspects of their lives, open the creative parts of their minds, and imagine the positive outcomes they can achieve in whatever endeavor they take on and whatever goals they set. I basically tell them to *quit* robbing themselves of the time and the ability to think, plan, and grow.

As I grew up on the farm and then in my military time, I was a less-than-patient person. I wanted to get the chore done and complete the mission. It frustrated me when someone would say, "Let's sleep on it." I felt this was a waste of time, and it seemed to merely push the next thing to do further down the road. I found that in most cases, we made better decisions, had more comprehensive plans, and operated more safely and efficiently. We basically learned how to *quit* effectively and make it a positive event.

Taking time to think before acting offers several advantages over simply continuing with an action. Here are some of the key benefits:

1. *Better decision-making:* When we take time to think things through, we can weigh the pros and cons of different options, anticipate potential risks and consequences, and make more informed decisions. This can lead to better outcomes and fewer regrets.
2. *Improved problem-solving:* When faced with a difficult problem, it can be tempting to jump straight into action in the

hopes of finding a solution quickly. However, taking time to think about the problem from different angles, brainstorming potential solutions, and considering alternative approaches can help us find more effective and creative solutions.
3. *Reduced impulsivity:* Acting impulsively can lead to rash decisions and actions that we may later regret. By taking time to think before acting, we can reduce our impulsivity and make more deliberate and thoughtful choices.
4. *Increased self-awareness:* When we take time to reflect on our thoughts, feelings, and actions, we gain a better understanding of ourselves and our motivations. This can help us identify patterns of behavior that may be holding us back, and it can help us make positive changes to improve our lives.
5. *Enhanced emotional regulation:* Taking time to think can also help us regulate our emotions more effectively. When we act impulsively, our emotions can often get the best of us. However, by taking a step back and giving ourselves time to think, we can better manage our emotions and respond in more productive and constructive ways.

LESSONS FROM THE FIFTEEN-MINUTE QUITTER

- Quit long enough to give yourself time to be successful.
- Taking a pause will save you money and more.
- Allow your team to quit for fifteen minutes or longer; they will pay you back tenfold.
- Even a long, deep breath is a form of good quitter time; take one.
- Thinking about your task before you execute it lets you make mistakes before they become real.

Leaders Pick Up Their Own Shit First

When you grow up in rural America, you tend to live in a fishbowl. It can be a wonderful fishbowl with close relationships, help from an extended community when you need it, and a familiarity with your surroundings that makes you feel comfortable and, in some ways, safe. The flip side is that you are very close so everyone can see everything. They see who you date, what you are doing, and where you are going. People know who you hang out with and if you are "good" or "bad." They can see your literal and proverbial front yard. They notice anything and everything, and, yes, they comment on it. Often, they will pass judgment based on what they see—I call this throwing rocks.

Most of the farms where I grew up were well-kept, showed a lot of pride, and reflected well on the farmer. However, there was always a farm or two that, when others drove by or stopped in, looked like it wasn't well kept or the animals were not as well cared for as others. One's immediate thought might be that this was a bad or irresponsible farmer, right? The farmer was sloppy, and in some odd way, it makes others feel better to talk about the farmer as if they were an example of what not to do. People may throw verbal "rocks" at the farmer. Not in his or her presence but usually to the crowd at the diner or the bar. However, people may talk about the farmer without knowing what in the world was *really* going on at the farm. We all need to *quit* throwing rocks.

In my thirty years of service, one event played out in the same way as I've just described. We were in a small unit, a family atmosphere, with a feeling of being cared for and safe. Everyone knew their stuff. We had rock throwers, and many of them had a motive or a reason—whether or not it was poorly motivated. STOP HERE: I will admit right now that I was a rock thrower, and I am not proud of it. After I learned a few things, I *quit*. When I corrected someone in uniform, it amazed me how they would react, and this little ritual made me stop throwing rocks.

Rock throwing is the ultimate sign of disrespect, shallow leadership, or poor personal management in life. Rock throwers bypass gathering data; they don't stop to find out the truth but rather make assumptions and conclusions that can be hurtful or even permanently damaging to reputations, self-confidence, and trust. Many of the rocks thrown revolved around correcting something on a uniform that was incorrect. It goes like this: "Excuse me, you need to adjust your gig line" (the line made by your shirt down to your pants and buckle), or "Your name tag is crooked." It never failed to produce the same reaction over thirty years. The person you are correcting immediately looks at your gig line or your name tag to make sure you are squared away as well. They are looking to see if you have dog poop in your yard while you tell them to pick up theirs.

As I gained more responsibility and was in positions that required leadership, I started to see how damaging rock throwers are in an organization or a community. They drive gossip—most of which is partly true, at best. This has to be mitigated, and you cannot be guilty of the same. It is more difficult than you know. Most only stop throwing rocks when they become the target. They are hurt and damaged and then they start to find grace.

The farmer's story may end like this: "Did you know he has been battling cancer for a year now, has struggled financially because of it, and doesn't have any help?" So is he really a bad farmer? Did he deserve the pain of the stones thrown his way? Was the damage reparable? To truly lead, to truly be a person others trust and follow, we must not throw rocks. We need to clean up our own dog poop first—not so you have permission to throw rocks but so you can grow, develop, and mentor from a position of a good example. If you have ever been in a rock fight, you remember the rock you threw was the one the other guy picked up and threw back to hit you. With that, I leave you with a few lessons and thoughts on how to *quit* throwing rocks and up your game.

Throwing rocks only hurts people, and that's not where you want to be. It is so easy to lean into assumptions or act out against a perceived issue in a literal or figurative violent way. We use words and actions to lash out at people when we don't have a full understanding of the context for why certain behaviors take place. When we throw rocks, they hurt. Such rocks may drive people, and those who follow you, to not only quit but to make decisions with much worse consequences. I am not saying we shouldn't give constructive feedback. Sometimes doing that is a great leader trait. But it may also hurt feelings, and sometimes the reaction is to throw a rock back. It comes in all directions. Rock throwing is never productive. Feedback is tough; rock throwing is wrong. Leaders quickly become lonely when they throw rocks and, more importantly, when they let rock throwing happen. Rock throwing is a sign, just like the cows all lying down.

LESSONS FOR ROCK THROWERS

- Rock damage can destroy families and organizations.
- Don't step over and ignore the poop in your yard; those following you can see it.
- When you experience rock throwing, how do you handle it? Stop it, or shy away?
- When you feel yourself picking up a rock, STOP and ask the person if there is a way you can help.
- The energy used to throw rocks can be better spent helping the neighbor clean up poop.
- Positive change is never achieved through rock throwing.
- Check your gig line before you correct someone else's.

Quit Being a Tough Person

How do being lonely and *quitting* correlate? Well, let's ask a question and tell a story. Do you feel lonely as a leader? Like nobody understands you? The burden of leadership is heavy. You may be reminding yourself that "Nobody understands my responsibility" or "The buck stops here." This may all be true to an extent, and it can cause stress. But it should never cause loneliness. I have met people, worked for people, and led people who I wanted to grab by the shoulders and shout out to them, "STOP being lonely! Please find help and *quit* being a sad sack or martyr."

The story here is about asking for help. Doing so requires you to be courageous and put your ego aside. You have to realize that what you are going through probably isn't novel or the first time ever. On the farm, the farmer is responsible for everything. If the farmer is fortunate enough, they can afford to hire a worker or two to help with chores, but farmers usually do most of the work by themselves in order to save money and time. Many, of course, probably go it alone because they want the work done their way (the right way). I remember times when I would hear farmers say, "I need help." Recently, it played out in a way that was a show of leadership and humility for all of us to learn.

Unlike the farms where I grew up in California, the Montana farms have different dynamics. We have cold and snow, and sometimes a lot of snow. I have been fortunate enough to make some true friends since moving to Montana in 2014, and a few of them are farmers. This past winter, we had a few bad storms that dropped several feet of snow during calving times. Most cattle ranchers in Montana breed their cows to have their babies in January through March, and this requires a lot of work and long days. The advantages of the calves being born in the dead of winter far outweigh the danger to them, and the farmer works hard to keep the moms warm as the calves are born to ensure they are both protected and the newborns do well. I have even witnessed seasoned ranchers put one or two calves in the front of the truck with the heater on to keep them warm. Some have even been known to take them into the house. It is amazing and a true sign of selflessness and leading.

This past winter, my farmer friend was in a part of Montana that got hit hard with storms right in the middle of calving season. I know this guy, and he is tough and well-known in this part of North Dakota and Montana. He usually had help from his sons and family, but this storm isolated him, his farm, and the community. I knew he was probably in a hard spot, and it was getting tough on him and the calves. I reached out and simply said, "If I can help, let me know." I was not expecting to hear back because he was very busy and probably had a great plan. Well, the next thing I knew, a text dinged and my phone rang. This hardened farmer, who everyone thought had it all figured out and could weather any storm (literal or figurative), asked for help. Their property was blocked by the snow, they were low on colostrum (the milk that moms usually pass along to help the immune systems of the calves), and he needed me to bring some if I could get through on the roads. My respect went way up for my friend. He chose not to be lonely but rather to share his "pain" without being coy about it; he just said he needed help. The situation was extremely bad and the roads impassable, but he saved a high percentage of animals. They made it through the event, not unscathed but whole, and his asking for help was key to a large portion of their survival.

As leaders, it is easy to compartmentalize your challenge of the week, day, year, or beyond. You can hold it in and be "tough" and whine about how rough you have it, or you can share and let your challenge be a part of someone's life who can be of help—this is a "tool" you need to add to your life kit.

As I was privileged enough to watch some fine leaders during my career and into these post-retirement years, it amazes me to watch them pick one of two ways to do things. Many instances come to mind, and I'll share this one.

When I was at a large organization, we had far too many deaths among our civilian force. We started to hold somber meetings that required us to ask why and to explore potential organizational norms that may have contributed to the devastating outcomes for people. I never enjoyed the programmatic approach to any of these, whether it was a motorcycle fatality, an accident due to poor safety, or suicide. I would try to work from an empathy level as I thought about each individual perspective from the data I knew. I found that when people left subtle messages prior to suicide, they had some common themes: they felt lonely, they had lost hope in something, they believed they were out of options to get and receive help, and whatever challenge they faced had become so overwhelming that they felt they only had one choice. Somewhere in there, they started feeling lonely and couldn't find a way to ask for help.

As I grew in leadership positions, I made a rule: I would create an environment where people could ask me for help. I showed that I cared enough so people would come to me with a challenge and give me the opportunity to affect their lives in a way that alleviated the loneliness, provided a constant outlet as they walked a tough journey, and meant just being present. I will tell you this wasn't, and isn't, easy for me, hence why I share these thoughts. To this point, I made myself vulnerable by sharing my own past failures and then being present through thick and thin. You can't say it and not do it, and the follow-through kept my team whole. There was no quitting in this environment.

If you think about a time when a situation didn't go well, we say, "Why didn't you ask for help?" My farmer friend asked for help before the calves died or when the issue at hand had progressed to a poor state. He was comfortable enough to do that, and the mantra is that there's no loss of pride in asking.

This leader loneliness is not necessary. I hope we all can find a way to shape our internal talk and encourage ourselves to ask for help when feeling lonely, when needing a hand, or when establishing the ability to keep an environment that makes those who may need you feel as if you are a great person with whom to share and work through challenges in life and leadership.

LESSONS ABOUT LONELINESS

- *Quit* being lonely, and build a network of help and understanding for you and your followers.
- "Tough" makes you lonely—that is probably your own fault.
- Keep running the help lines in life—somebody can make a difference or help—don't *quit*.
- When you say, "Why didn't you ask for help?" there is more to be done than fixing the immediate issue—a relationship needs to be improved.
- Loneliness breeds loss of hope—don't be lonely.
- If you feel lonely, fix it immediately. It stunts your growth and can hurt you.

If You Want to Be a Leader, You Must First Have Followers

I often hear statements such as, "I am the leader of the XYZ organization."

It always makes me wonder, "What do your people call you?" As you know, I grew up in agriculture and in the ag community, where Mother Nature is the leader. She takes you to places you may not want to go. She causes you to do things you wish didn't need to occur—but you follow her, you listen to what she says, you accept the hand you are given, and you use her traits and strengths to your advantage as you work with the challenges she puts in your way. Mother Nature teaches and helps you grow. She also builds character. Why do we follow Mother Nature? One would argue that we have no choice; we can't control the wind, we certainly can't control the rain or the snow, and the temperature is what it is. So why do we look at the weather forecast or the sky or the temperature as we navigate our lives?

Mother Nature has built a team of followers by exhibiting a few key traits. **Honesty** is there for sure; when she says, "Rain," it rains, and when she says, "Wind," it is windy, so she is **Reliable**. She provides what is needed for the farmer and for all of us in the forms of sun, water, and temperatures to grow—she **Provides** resources. She is always on time and **Present**. She **Challenges** and **Grows** her followers in many ways, and allows you to **Learn**.

I have worked for and with some tremendous leaders, both in my days as a farm kid and as a military leader and Airman. I have also worked for some people in leadership positions who never got it; they thought they were in charge and wouldn't believe anything people thought about them or did to them. Their "leadership" was the opposite of anything resembling a respectful leader. Let me set the stage for a few stories. See if you know these types of people. They are the ones who say, "I am in charge now, so listen to me." They ask condescending questions like "Do you know who I am?" They state their superiority, boasting, "I am in charge of this company, squadron, etc., so you will listen to me!" And my favorite example and most exasperating person is the one who says, "From my position, I see it this way, and you are not here, so there is nothing you can tell me or contribute that I don't already know."

In 2008, I was in Iraq acting as the Chief of the trauma center. At the time, my Colonel (this man was an absolutely tremendous leader, my friend, and my running buddy) left for R&R. He was replaced by his deputy commander. I worked with this new Colonel, and he was nothing special, nor was he, in my eyes, someone who wowed me as a leader. Up until this time, he had been inert and followed directions from my Colonel. Then the monster in him was released.

My boss got on the plane, and as soon as the wheels went up, this Colonel turned into the man with the power. And boy, did he let us know it! At this time, we had a lot going on in our unit. One of the keystone issues we had been working on was getting a young Iraqi orphan adopted by a family in the United States. We worked hard to safely get her to the US and settled into her new home with a new family. This endeavor had press coverage, and the messages about any sensitive issues had been developed over time to ensure no miscommunications. My boss had been the center of all that.

Then comes this Colonel. He had not kept up with the issue, and he was poorly educated on the local culture and cultural norms, such as how to handle the press, and he apparently didn't know how to let the people who had actually done the work handle the issue. He was in charge now, and he was going to be on camera. Ironically, his plan was to get this issue across the finish line so he could take credit for all of it. This one act, and his subsequent actions, caused him to lose the entire team as they left him to fail and would only follow him under duress. This Colonel was *not* a leader since he had no followers.

The situation needed to be addressed with the general in charge, where the Colonel would be assessed to see if he was worthy of holding the responsibilities. I was asked about him and his authority problem; the general and his vice commander were both wanting to know my take on the issue. Initially, I said, "I am not comfortable throwing my senior officers under the bus." To which my general replied, "Chief, sometimes people crawl under the bus with no help at all." He was right, and the issues were corrected to preserve the health and well-being of our command and mission. I would love to hear this guy's portrayal of this story today.

Have you ever had someone tap their name tag or say, "Do you know who I am?" How does that make you feel? I bet that makes you less likely to want to follow the person. I remember a non-leader at my worst assignment in my Air Force time. She almost cost me a long career. She was enamored with her position and title, and she definitely felt threatened by anyone who challenged her or had other ideas (often that was me, unfortunately). Her response was to remind people she was in charge or condescendingly remind them of her rank.

A few years later, after I had left, I went back to this place to visit friends. Lo and behold, I ran into this "leader." I had a bunch more stripes by this point, and a pretty cool position. I had never thought I would see her again. When she saw me, she asked how I was doing and what I was doing. I gave a quick answer, and she looked at me, turned sideways, and with a smile, tapped her new rank from a recent promotion. It took all I had to not comment, as I knew that would be her last promotion; her time was shorter than she knew—she had failed her followers. They had left her, and she was left to flounder until she quit the job and the Air Force. Sadly, it was her incompetence that led to her losing many good people because she never had any respect for those who could have made her brilliant. Her lack of followers, in the end, was the downfall of her and her career.

One of my worst moments as a leader, one which took some time to recover from, involved a long, bad day in an emergency room in Japan. I had a great team there, and I tried hard to let them grow without too much of "my way or the highway." I was learning and practicing patience, and part of my self-improvement was to let the team grow through their ideas and processes. I didn't disengage completely, but instead I let them learn and grow without damaging anything.

One of my strategies was to pass on the skills I knew how to do well or in an expert manner so others could master those tasks and responsibilities. This worked well sometimes, and other times it was interrupted as I passed along my work knowledge. I was learning, and they were too. However, on this day, I damaged myself as a leader. It was a simple moment in time within a chaotic emergency room (ER). The ER has highly competent people doing important work, and when it gets tense and the volume gets high, it requires you to be direct in nature to get things done quickly and efficiently.

In my opinion, directive leadership should be held for these times and used sparingly; this was a time that required it. To be directive, you need to have built trust and solid relationships. If this foundation isn't set and you become directive, you may get a response you didn't expect or one that is counter to the goals and mission. On this day, I found out that one of my Staff Sergeants wasn't sold on me or my leadership, or maybe I had not earned his respect. I was oblivious to this, and as this situation unfolded, I was needed to lead directly and take charge. The rest of the team was doing well, and the Sergeant was not a bad performer or a problem; in fact, he was a shift leader—an important job. We needed to move things, including patients and vehicles. This was shortly after 9/11, and we had recently been informed of some concerning intelligence.

As I was developing the plan, I "told" (not asked) the Sergeant to go get the keys to a number of vehicles because we had to move certain vehicles to the front of the facility and reorganize patients and patient rooms. At the time, he was stressed with other issues, and I wasn't sensitive to that. Plus, we needed to get this work done quickly. I did what all good leaders do, right? I repeated the order out loud and basically said move out. He turned on me, looked me straight in the eye, and rattled off a pile of tasks he had to do. He complained that he felt what we were doing was stupid, and he wanted to know why we were doing this. In my most seasoned leadership tone, I retreated to position power. I looked him in the eye and said, "Because I told you so, and I am your superior." I knew I screwed up before the last word crossed my lips, but they were out of my mouth, and the damage was done. I had some serious work to do. Later, our relationship turned out okay, but I was wrong and my words were unnecessary.

I had the opportunity to be in the presence of many high-ranking Air Force leaders while attending meetings in conference rooms and boardrooms to discuss the development, sustainability, and future of the Air Force. During this time, I observed some leaders I knew well lose the trust and support of their followers. One reason for this was their tendency to dismiss the perspectives of their subordinates so they could emphasize their own high-level views. This behavior, epitomized by the statement, "You need to pull yourself up from the ten-thousand-foot view to the thirty-thousand-foot view where I am at," damaged the Air Force's culture and caused many to lose faith in their leaders. As a result, these individuals, though holding leadership positions, failed to effectively lead, and they lost the respect and trust of their followers, including me.

LESSONS ON HAVING FOLLOWERS

- To have followers, they must respect you—do they? How do you know?
- Position power never builds or sustains followership—what are you using?
- Building followership and having followers require a relationship and trust. That is your work; are you doing it?
- Good followers help their leaders fill gaps and grow—are you a good follower?
- Are you healthy for your team, or are you climbing under the bus? What do your followers think?
- If your followers are leaving, do you look at them, or do you look in the mirror first?
- What can you learn from Mother Nature? Do you enjoy the challenge?
- If you think you may have lost your followers—you have. You better get to work.
- People care about being respected and heard, not about the letter in your signature block.

Get Over Yourself—*Quit* Flexing in the Mirror

Growing up in small-town America is cool, and sometimes you get to learn lessons early on in life. One thing everyone learns at a young age is that you better get over yourself—and quickly! On the farm, the other boys and I thought we were the toughest, strongest, and best at everything. The ladies mostly worked in the house, where they cooked and cleaned, and they also tended to a few chores that were outside and in the heat. They had to take it all the fruits of the garden after walking the "hots rocks" of outside chores.

It only takes a hot summer day, bare feet (we were always without shoes), and a small challenge before the lessons of life come right to the front. Our farm in Northern California usually experienced pretty good weather, but if you have ever been in that valley in the middle of the summer, you know how hot it is—110 degrees and more can be common, with a dip merely into the nineties at night. Nothing cools off, and anything made of asphalt or cement is downright dangerous. The smell of cool well water hitting that hot cement still makes me cringe to this day. The best way to describe it is just plain old *hot*.

When on the farm, you have a lot of gravel—gravel for the driveways, pathways, and in areas you don't want to mow. These gravel areas are not for the weak. You must be strong, move quickly, and run fast on it with your bare feet (or put shoes on, for crying out loud, kid!). We all did it, and we all paid the price in scorched soles. The hot rocks and the running around made us, in some way, stronger, tougher, and ready for anything—in fact, I was the toughest and baddest of them all, right? In my mind, at least, I was all that and a bag of chips.

Then I made a mistake. I told my gramps I was the fastest and baddest kid ever on the hot gravel; nobody could beat me. Gramps was probably thinking, "This kid needs to get over himself." He said, "I bet your cousin can beat you." Michelle is smaller than me despite being two years older. But she is obviously faster, so I think he knew the result before he even proceeded to teach me to get over myself. To make it interesting, he incentivized the event and set the rules: best two out of three to the barn and back, and you must touch the barn. They might have been other obligatory rules you have to spell out for children.

This was going to be easy! She was the girl, and I was the boy; outcome resolved before they even said go. The prize was a nickel to the winner. We lined up, and the "Ready, set, go!" was called. Off we went, running on hot rocks. I will spare you the suspense because this doesn't end like Hollywood; it was a drubbing. I was a mile behind and hobbling as my cousin smoked me badly. I wasn't happy, and my ego was pretty bruised—thank goodness my gramps did that to me because I had to, at some point, get over myself.

Roll the clock forward to a time when I was taking on leadership roles. I also had leaders above me, and I watched with interest their different styles. In one assignment, I had a pair of leaders who could never get over themselves. They were enamored with the way they looked in the mirror, their rank, and their position; meanwhile, they constantly reminded you of who they thought they were and why that made them better. (Not unlike a drunk actor saying to a cop after being pulled over, "Do you know who I am?")

This was the worst assignment I had experienced in thirty years. We had careerist leaders who could not get over themselves long enough to care for and feed the rest of us. They had decided *they* were the best, *they* had the most rank, and *nobody* could touch them. This all played out in a way I wish it had not, but here you go.

My wife was still active-duty Air Force serving as a nurse, and she was pregnant with our first son. I was finishing up a remote tour as an Independent Medic (similar to a Physician's Assistant, but all by yourself and a long way away from any other help). I was leaving England to be with her and to join my new team. My son was born in July, and I arrived in August. We had a new family, new jobs, and a new routine. The place we worked was a large teaching hospital with many highly experienced people. Some did similar work to my remote medicine specialty I described; however, there is a twist.

The training and clinical work required to maintain certifications are time consuming and can be overwhelming, but they are extremely necessary so you are ready to "go" at a moment's notice. This hospital was a mecca for training, as it had everything and every opportunity to get lots of experience. Here I was, a new dad, the new guy in town, trying to get settled in a new marriage and fatherhood, and I got a call one day while I was off duty (it is never a good call when you are off duty). The Chief called and told me, "We have a tasking to go to Somalia. It is for sixty days, maybe more. We want you to go. Are you willing and able to do that?"

A couple of details play into this. One, I wasn't allowed to deploy within forty-five days of arriving at a new assignment. And two, if I did get a waiver, I was leaving my wife and kiddo again just after being reunited with them. I responded to the Chief, "I know there are at least five others who can go; they are independent medics too." His response was shocking. He said, "You are right, Dave; however, none of them are current in certification and training." Pause this thought for a moment and come back to the farm with me.

My cousin had obviously been barefoot more than me, ran more than me, and was just faster. (If you remember from my first book, I can't run fast anyway.) She was prepared, she was better trained, and she had the ability. Most of all, she was able to withstand the hot rocks better than I could.

As I stood there in my kitchen listening to the Chief say he would have another base and person take the tasking, I reflected on the situation and thought, "What does this make my new organization look like? What does it say about me if I don't step up? Some of my peers need to take their shoes off and start running on hot rocks tomorrow."

So, I raised my hand and volunteered. What I didn't realize was that while I was gone, changes would happen, and I was certainly in for a surprise after I got back. I had started a new culture. I had made an entire institution relook at their priorities through my selflessness of doing the right thing. By stepping up for the team and going (to a place, let's just say, not very accommodating), I also was indirectly forcing a large group that had become comfortable with their status in the institution to get over themselves, realize they were not all that, and stop looking—and flexing—in the mirror.

As I departed on the trip, I didn't know that fellow independent medics were immediately being put into training, a program was restarted, and expectations reestablished. They were never going to have to hold the conversation again. What came next, however, was what I found most interesting in the leadership dynamic. There is an old saying, "Some people think their sh*t doesn't stink." Funny how, when truly present, this simple concept can destroy organizations and leaders' reputations.

As I mentioned, I had a couple of leaders who couldn't get away from the mirror. They certainly had success, as they were at the top or near it, but they were responsible for the failure of the program.

They were the ones who made the call—to me—to ask if I would go. They certainly thought their sh*t didn't stink.

I returned on time to my home and family, but in that short time away, a lot had happened, and I had some challenging moments. One of those moments inspired some of my Army buddies, with whom I was stationed, to put me and a few others in for a decoration. The decoration read like this:

CITATION TO ACCOMPANY THE AWARD OF

THE AIR FORCE COMMENDATION MEDAL
(THIRD OAK LEAF CLUSTER)

TO

DAVID R. NORDEL

Staff Sergeant David R. Nordel distinguished himself by outstanding achievement as the Independent Duty Medical Technician, 1610 Air Logistic Support Group Forward, Mogadishu, Somalia, from 8 October 1993 to 1 December 1993. While deployed in support of Operation RESTORE HOPE II, a humanitarian relief effort in Somalia, Sergeant Nordel risked his life by voluntarily traveling 10 miles through unfriendly territory to provide life saving emergency treatment and evacuation of an Army sergeant who was trapped and critically injured in an overturned fuel truck. Furthermore, he skillfully treated hundreds of patients under austere field conditions, expertly coordinated 10 urgent aeromedical evacuations providing a life line to definitive care, meticulously maintained the forward messing facility to the highest health standards through vigilant inspections, and provided oversight for the processing of potable water for the 3,000 personnel assigned. The distinctive accomplishments of Sergeant Nordel reflect credit upon himself and the United States Air Force.

The result was a note from a two-star general that said, "We should attach a 'V' device for valor." By today's standards, my action may not seem too significant; however, at that time, we had not fought in many wars; we were still coming out of the Cold War. This note from the general started a reaction within those who didn't know their sh*t had odor, and they didn't truly understand what had happened to me when I was gone! They couldn't get over themselves. These "leaders" decided that they would make a case that the general was misguided and for the "V" not to be considered.

They won this fight, and the "V' was never awarded. I wasn't happy; in fact, I was pissed, but I quickly realized that it wasn't going to be productive to pursue that cause. We had bigger fish to fry, and that situation would remain a memory and not a reality. Why did I choose to pass this along in a book about "good quitting?" I think the lessons go like this.

LESSONS FROM GET OVER YOURSELF

- Do the right thing and "unquit," and worry about all that is wrong later.
- Fix the wrong by doing what is right—don't let others *quit*.
- If you think your sh*t doesn't stink, you better phone a friend before your reputation takes an irreversible hit—people will *quit* you.
- They only way to quickly run on hot rocks is to actually run on hot rocks.
- When you are posing in front of the mirror, you are getting weaker—*quit* it!
- Your actions in a difficult situation can change whole environments—think about whether it is for the good or the bad.

Does It Always Have to Be Your Idea?

Ideas either come to you directly (original ideas) or come from others (borrowed thoughts); sometimes these are such good ideas that people patent them and protect them for their value. People share some ideas so that others may prosper in some way. I argue that every idea is not good or bad, but the creative thought required for ideas is healthy and is usually centered on making life better—I am all for that! We may have entered a time, however, when putting effort into forming original ideas is a lost art, and it is making us weaker.

When you grow up in a farm community, many people have new ideas, especially when times are tough and economics add stress to the farm or the community. It amazed me to listen to seasoned farmers chat about the latest challenge, drought, or cattle prices. They all have new ideas or old ideas they have tried. They share them liberally, and, even though most won't admit it unless you really pick at them about it, they try many of these ideas. The idea may even become part of their new way of doing things. I also watched farmers give credit to those who gave them an idea or a better way of doing a task—they don't make it sound like it was their own idea (most of the time). There is magic in all this because in a small town, inevitably, it will come full circle and somebody will know whose idea it really was to begin with.

When I first retired from the Air Force, I took on a few new adventures and experiences. As I journeyed across a couple new work and personal environments, I was actively ingrained in critical thought, idea-making, and process and personal improvement. I was using the skills I had as I tried to change my environments for the positive to lead through the "drought" and "poor crop seasons" in life. What I had to learn quickly in this post-military world was that this way of thinking is not common practice. A phenomenon existed outside of the military that was tough for me to learn, and it was an area of improvement we all can work on. It's what my mother would call "Cutting off your nose to spite your face." I had entered a world where creative thought and ideas were not welcome; they were met with major resistance and given the "hand," per se.

I jumped into my post-military life with the viewpoint that the people, processes, and systems in the civilian world were similar and predicated on commonalities such as mutual respect, respect for expertise, and truth telling. What I found was an environment in which critical and strategic thought had become a threat, and people and organizations were worried about looking bad because they personally or corporately hadn't thought of a recently presented process, idea, or way. The reaction to suggestions of change, or the introduction of a new way to do things based on experience, was discounted and, at times, squashed by a leader or system through position power or threat of job loss.

Why do I put this out there, and what does it have to do with *quitting*? A story or two come to mind that, to this day, baffle me. I was called on just before Memorial Day to be on an incident command team that was preparing for a potential flood that would require the evacuation of over three thousand people. As we formed, this small cadre of people had decided (through a critical thought process) that we needed to open shelters, contact the people who could be affected, and preposition certain details as we continued to get briefings on the weather. We had a solid plan put together by the subject-matter experts, but what came next was unnatural to me and stopped me in my tracks.

After the elected officials and decision-makers walked into the room and took the briefing of the work we had done, one of them said, "This is Memorial Day weekend, nobody will be here to handle this, and it probably won't flood, anyway." What!? I was shocked and sat in dismay. Over the holiday, the four of us on this incident command team sat there and prepared a community for the flood and worked to protect them. Then it hit me like jumping in an ice-cold lake; it was so counterintuitive to anything that made sense to me, and it all came down to the fact that it wasn't their idea. They didn't trust subject-matter expertise, and the decision was to do none of that because they would look weak or it may cost them votes. This is the same group of people that was responsible for this community during COVID and, most recently, another flood.

On the farm, if it had to be your idea and you never asked a question or never listened to others, your crops would fail and your animals would suffer. Frankly, if you can't do it all alone in farming, during a disaster, or even just while navigating life, then why would you maintain the mindset as a leader that you don't do something because it wasn't your idea—especially when it is for the greater good? In my previous writings, I have stated that knowledge is power only when shared. An idea that is not yours is an adjunct to being a respected and effective manager or leader, whether in your family or your career. So *quit* worrying about whose idea it was and start repeating the ideas of your experts (even if they are your children). Give credit and grow—you'll grow as a leader and be anointed as such.

If you picked up this book to see why people *quit* their leaders, here are a few reasons—I hope you find a nugget!

LESSONS FROM NOT YOUR IDEA!

- If you are the leader, the subject-matter experts make you smarter—don't fear them.
- Going it alone is lonely and does nothing but make you weaker.
- Ideas are what got us to the moon—do you think they all came from one person?
- People work hard in their subject-matter areas; let them "show off"—they have earned it.
- Share your ideas and help people; not sharing makes you weaker.
- If you want your family or your professional life to grow—solicit ideas and don't be afraid to try something new, odd, or unfamiliar.
- You are not the subject-matter expert in everything; you are probably not the subject-matter expert in most things—so don't act like it!
- If you have ideas and you are the subject-matter expert, yet others are not listening or they are discounting you, then I promise there are places and people that will appreciate you elsewhere. Work in a place that deserves you and build a family environment the same way.

Celebrate! Because If You Don't, That Genie Won't Go Back in the Bottle

We all have done something we wish we could take back: those are our genies. I'm willing to bet that most of your loose genies are probably because you didn't see the cows lying down.

As I write this chapter, it is my birthday—I am in Canada fishing with a dear friend who happens to be my guide. He has had recent challenges in life and is working hard to grow, change, and make himself better in all ways. As we have chatted for the last few days, he brought to mind a few qualities that are missing in our day-to-day lives and in our leadership roles. You see, on my birthday, and in my guide's life, we have opportunities to celebrate. Where do I put that in a book about *quitting*?—follow closely, and I'll lay it all out!

When I grew up in Orland, California, there was always a celebration going on, and they made special events for the community. These celebrations took many forms and revolved around different topics. In the summer, there was heat, and I really mean that it was *hot*! It was an alive time, with trips to Black Butte Lake to fish or learn to waterski—a sport I discovered that I am the worst at. The smell of eucalyptus was dominating near the county golf course as we drove down the country roads, and it made me feel safe. The morning was filled with the low coo of the doves as the dew on the hay and grass gave way to what would surely be a "scorcher."

The county fair in Orland each year was a major time in our lives. We had the parades—the livestock shows (I worked a summer there and cleaned every animal pen at least once), the family gatherings, and of course, the destruction derby (this was the crown jewel). Suffice it to say that Orland celebrates, and they do it well. What if all that stopped tomorrow; how would that look?

Being Portuguese here is a big deal, and our heritage is tied to all the reasons we party and celebrate during the summer—most of all, a traditional fiesta. This event is a happening, complete with authentic sopas, and the meat is to die for. All the families converged for a multi-day preparation that culminated in a huge celebration, bringing people from near and far. People literally stopped what they were doing and celebrated, partied, and otherwise enjoyed each other's company. The stresses of life were set aside while people danced the Chamarrita and put their cares on hold.

Did I mention that it was hot during this event? It was really hot, and those doing the work made it a true labor of love. It was the ultimate party! When I was young, this just seemed to be a ritual or simply that time of year again. It was fun, but I didn't have an appreciation for what the fiesta really was—it was to celebrate our heritage, our lives, and our friendships and family—it was a healthy pause we all needed, and it grounded us.

One would think I should be good at celebrating and pausing to acknowledge accomplishments. Well, not so much at times. I was driven, and hitting a home run was what we all were supposed to do. Time and effort were to be spent fixing something, hitting the next home run, and moving to the next area of need. That is production, that is outcome, and that is an increased bottom line, but that does *not* build satisfaction in a leader's followers, and it is not a good retention tool.

In early 2008, while in Iraq, I was taught a lesson that has served me well to this day—if you don't celebrate yourself, those around you, and the events that are important in a timely, genuine fashion, you will miss that opportunity, and that genie never gets back in the bottle. It just becomes a reference point for your followers to look back on when they are deciding whether you are leading or following. In the military, we celebrate formally and informally, including medal presentations or awards and sometimes birthday celebrations and office recognitions. But in Iraq, they took it a step further, and I hated it! What these thoughtful and brilliant followers and leaders came up with was the best and most appropriate celebration of accomplishment and people I have ever seen. It drove me crazy as I thought it was a waste of time, so I was a spectator at first. What these warriors decided was that they wanted to have a rodeo and a country parade right in the middle of a "war"—what were they thinking? The answer was they were proud of themselves, and they knew they needed to pause and turn off the stresses of the situation and have some fun. They wanted to celebrate!

A large portion of our team in Iraq came from San Antonio and the large Air Force facility there. That site is like the mecca of Air Force medicine; it has trained some very, very good professionals and staff! That group decided to reach out to a local radio station back home and see if they would sponsor this event, and boy, did they pull it off. This radio station sponsored the whole event; they sent pallets and pallets of shirts, trinkets, and just about anything we asked for. In turn, they all started the competitions: float building, rodeo queen and king, the mechanical bull ride, the parade and costume judging—this went on for days leading up to the event. I was walking through the trauma bay one day, and right in the middle of the bay was a giant float, and the doctor was riding in it—*What the hell is this?* I soon found out! This was a distraction, a fun diversion, and a way to reward themselves for a lot of hard, grueling, tough work. It was a celebration, not a waste of time, and I soon realized it was time well spent—a wake-up call to a gap in my leadership profile that needed to improve. A gap my followers were showing me—I appreciated it, and so I said, "This is really cool, now get the dang float out of the trauma bay!" No, I did not say that, but I thought it!

Well, the party went off without a hitch; the fun was incredible, and I was proud of what they had done. The benefits were important and beneficial, and they schooled up the old Chief!

When I returned from Iraq, I went to my first Command Chief job. One of my first requests to the staff was to identify significant dates for all of our enlisted Airmen. Most of them were focused on their anniversary in the Air Force or their promotion dates, so I made sure each one received a hand-signed note. How do you think that went? As I visited duty areas and work centers, I would see those small notes pinned in cubicles, on walls, and in dorm rooms and lockers, and I would always say, "I see you got my note!" The responses sounded like this: "Yes, Chief, that is awesome." "Thanks for remembering." And, the best of all, "I sent a copy to my mom or dad or family." This small act was so cheap (actually free, short of the paper we used), and the return on that investment is still paying off—simply by celebrating someone's accomplishments in life!

So today is my birthday, but we are not going to celebrate my annual day of birth. Instead, we are going to celebrate my friend and his fight with cancer, career, discoveries of what makes him happy, recent journeys, and triumphs and growth. We are going to have a festival to relax and leave the worries behind; we will catch and eat fresh walleye pulled from the lake that very day and have a fair, a festival, and a fiesta. We probably won't dance, but ice cream will be our joy! We will pause and appreciate each other and make sure we give ourselves the recognition we deserve. I wish I had learned this sooner, and even now, I am still learning it, but your growth as a leader once you learn to celebrate is a quantum leap. So try it! It feels good and recharges batteries! Don't ever get caught with this genie out of the bottle; it won't go back in! *Quit* being so driven, and remember to celebrate.

LESSONS FROM CELEBRATE

- Parties have a place—they are not a waste of time, so invest in them.
- Your followers are waiting in silence to be recognized, and they do care and are taking notes.
- You can't have a celebration of significance the day after it should have happened.
- Celebrate yourself too. It actually makes you feel good, and your people expect it.
- Leaders who don't celebrate have a gap to fill. I did, and it was a gift.
- Keep a notebook or electronic calendar of important dates and make sure you remember them—but be genuine; form letters and emails stink!

Nurses of Torrejon

This book talks about *quitting*, and in some ways, it may be about not starting something or not *quitting*. Some of the most powerful leaders in my life were the ones who didn't *quit*—not on me or themselves. My start in the United States Air Force was littered with non-*quitters*—they were the nurses of Torrejon.

When I was growing up, I wanted to be a plumber. Heck, I had a cousin who did it, and he made good money, so why not? Well, the Air Force made me a medic, and that decision exposed me to some of the most wonderful people and leaders I have ever known. I used to think I was lucky and they just found me, but now I realize that it was a combination of some of the greatest gifts I have ever been given.

As I grew up, a challenge was often ahead of me, and I had to learn to solve it quickly out of necessity. In Orland, California, as I mentioned, the summer is dreadfully hot. As I grew older and became a contributor to the daily activities it takes to run a farm or an orchard, I needed to be taught, learn, and execute tasks like operating a tractor or other equipment, how to get the pumps and tanks set up to do the milking, and how to clean it all up for the next milking. This required a few roles to ensure I did it right. One role is a trainer and leader, one is a cheerleader, and one is a mentor.

On one of those long summer days, I had two chores to accomplish: check squirrel traps for a neighbor, and drive their truck to do it (no air conditioning for me on this day). In the oppressive heat, I would learn to drive a manual transmission vehicle for the first time. My legs were finally long enough, and I was strong enough to handle the non-power steering that was part of this old rig. So, with the windows down, I was sitting in the driver's seat when my leader and trainer showed up. He explained how the truck worked and pointed out each of the pedals; he told me how the clutch worked and then reviewed some pointers on the best way to make it all come together. Then he said, "Now go check the traps."

Well, this is where the real learning began. If you have ever driven a manual transmission, you know how it goes. As I let out the clutch, the truck jumped forward and stalled. *Shoot*, I quickly remembered that I had to push the gas at the same time. Then the truck would wind up to a roar, I released the clutch in a clumsy manner, and the truck lurched forward again and stalled. Repeat this a few times and listen to the laughter of those watching.

Damn it, anyway! Then suddenly, the truck moved. It was going—hooray! And then it dawned on me that now I had to shift as the engine screamed from being in too low a gear. It was crying to be shifted to the higher gear, so I pushed in the clutch as the engine was still roaring. Grabbing the gear shift, I tried to get it into the gear I wanted—darn, I missed! It went into a gear that was too high, and as I let out the clutch, the truck died again—total frustration! Okay, Dave, take a deep breath and start over: clutch in, start the truck, put it in low gear, give it a little gas, and let off the clutch. Eventually, this smoothed out, and I quickly realized that you also need to look out the windshield and actually drive in a straight line. There certainly was a lot going on and a lot to learn through much trial and error. But I got there eventually. By the time I finished with the traps, I was doing pretty well and had gained some confidence.

I was thinking about this moment as I was introduced to the nurses of Torrejon.

When I left the farm and that instructor (the truck) and went on my way, I had no idea what I would face or how I would do when faced with new and scary opportunities, and I certainly didn't know who would be there when I needed help. Flying on TWA airlines from St. Louis to Madrid, Spain, was like living in a movie; none of it seemed real, and most certainly I could never predict any of what was in front of me. I remember looking out the window, seeing the coast of Portugal, and thinking, "My ancestors are from there, and I am scared to death and all alone." When you venture out in the world (or even just to check squirrel traps), you hope and pray that you find someone to give you a hand and get you started on the right path and, most of all, keep you safe from the big bad world. I wish I could say I was brave and full of confidence, but not so much. As I walked out of the airport, I heard a voice say loudly, "Airman Nordel!" and it was like a big comfy blanket; somebody was picking me up and was going to keep me safe. This was my sponsor; he was a guy who would become a lifelong friend, and even today, we chat about this part of my journey.

Once settled with a room, a roommate (another lifelong friend), and instructions on where to report and to whom, I was feeling a bit better about my basic needs. But now I had to go be a medic. I had to fight to get the job I wanted. I was shown around the hospital, and we walked in the areas where I could be assigned. After seeing every area, I asked to work on the OB/GYN floor. It had forty beds, and twenty were in an open bay that did labor and delivery, nursery care, and gynecology services and surgeries. What was I thinking? If I was nervous about work, I just made it double hard. This was a world better navigated by female medics and registered nurses. I begged to be placed there, and they obliged me. Off I went to deliver babies. My first few days set the tone for a year of being led, taught, and developed in a way that gave me a foundation that, to this day, I still rely on.

This floor had one very long hallway. In the hallway were doors going to patient rooms and offices, and the nursery was at the end of the hall. It was a giant room that we called a bay, and it contained beds only separated by pull curtains. It was the largest hospital in this region and handled all pregnancies for the military families across this part of Europe. My first stop at work was to the office of my non-commissioned officer in charge (NCOIC)—these are the experienced enlisted men and women. He was to welcome me, make sure I had everything I needed, and start my training progression. He assigned me a trainer (another lifelong friend) and introduced me around the unit.

One fact about being an enlisted medic is that you work mainly with officers, as the nurses and doctors are all officers, along with many of the key staff. So, unlike most other units, it can have more officers than enlisted. As a new Airman, this was intimidating with all the "yes ma'am," "no ma'am," "yes sir," "stand at parade," and "rest" exchanges. The uncomfortable environment was soon neutralized by the people who would become my teammates; my fellow medics and the nurses of Torrejon. They had names like Charlotte, Brenda, Maria, and Lisa, but I called them ma'am, captain, or lieutenant.

These people (I forget a name or two because I am old) became my first leaders. They had this brand-new kid (me), full of energy (I told my NCOIC that I would be the best he ever had on day one) and ready to go, and they were the catalysts to how this went. My trainer, George, was one of the non-commissioned officers, and he was great. George showed me the ropes, made sure I had the basics, and taught me some tricks of the trade. I am forever grateful for and to him.

One day came, sooner than I expected, when George said, "You are on the schedule alone." No more top cover from George—just me and two of these nurses, officers, scary people with education, and all the answers—or so I thought. They became my new team, and I was their new teammate. I knew one thing for sure: this place could get extremely busy. It could get to a point where everyone was maxed out with work, we could deliver a bunch of babies at once, and we could have a twelve-hour shift from hell. Case in point, on Super Bowl night in 1985, when the Bears and Patriots were playing, I was going to watch the game if the unit was slow. So, I set up a room with a TV and put a chair in there. By the time I got back to the nurse's station, the first of many laboring moms came in. I never saw a single play of the game. The ladies, officers, leaders, and nurses demonstrated what I call caring, compassionate, no-nonsense leadership. They respected me, they trained me, and they expected me to do certain tasks and exhibit certain qualities. In turn, they had my back. They truly cared about us as their followers, their medics (technicians), and valued team members. Mostly, though, they didn't accept excuses—not even an excuse of someone not knowing something.

One day not long after George let me go into the world all on my own, I was working with a nurse named Charlotte. To me, she was intimidating, tough, and super smart, but on this day, as far as she was concerned, we were the two people charged with taking care of a ward full of people. I learned quickly in nursing that the patient and I always had one desire in common—we wanted to discharge them, and the patient wanted to go home. Once the doctor said, "I am discharging XYZ patient," the process began. The patient would be ready to go immediately, and the staff had a pile of charting, IV lines to discontinue, other tubes and wires to disconnect, and did I mention the charting?—ugh. So, Charlotte says to me in the middle of a very busy time, "Please run down and take out Mrs. X's Foley catheter." (A Foley catheter is the tube that drains the bladder.) As I heard her direction, she must have noticed the look on my face, and she immediately followed up with, "What!?" My response would send me on a learning adventure that showed her teaching was done out of truly caring about me, my progression, and strengthening our team.

I said, "I don't know how to do that."

She replied, "Why not?"

I explained, "Nobody has ever shown me how."

This turned my nurse into a tomato, and it scared me to death as she turned red, spun around, grabbed some supplies, and said, "Come with me." She pulled me into the room with her, explained to the patient what we were going to do, and said that she was training me. She proceeded to take the catheter out as I watched and learned. Once complete, we went back to the nurses' station, where she said (still a bit red in the face), "Don't you ever tell me again you don't know how to do something. Tell me so we can teach you." This is a statement she grew to regret (no, really) because anything I wanted to do and didn't know how to do, I told her. In no time at all, I was doing almost everything I could and was really contributing as a team member. I wondered if she was one-of-a-kind or if it was like that with all the nurses. To my pleasure, I would get the gift of training from all the nurses and medics senior to me. It put me on a path to success and also taught me valuable lessons.

Leaders can choose various responses to the statement, "I don't know how to do it." My nurses of Torrejon chose to stop, invest in me, and not *quit* on the new Airman and medic! The results of those decisions paid off for everyone!

These are special people who made such an impact on me. I finished nursing school and love to teach today—I owe them all immensely.

LESSONS FROM NURSES

- What if I had said nothing and just jumped in the truck and faked it?
- Don't be afraid to ask for help or say you don't know how.
- Fight for training, and let people you trust mold you.
- When it is your turn to hear, "I don't know how to do it," will you respond like my nurse did?
- It is easier to just do it yourself—but it does nothing to improve the team or the future.
- Who is your "George" in life and leadership? Thank them; they deserve it.
- If you are a leader, bring people with you—the results multiply, enhance your team, and benefit your product and customer (or patient).
- When the boss's face turns red, it is not always a bad sign; it may just be their passion for excellence.

Can a Medic Build a Bomb or Fix an Airplane?

On a farm, there is always something to do; some of it requires a good, strong back, and other tasks require a bit more skill. The farm has many types of equipment, including some that take much learning and practice. It takes all parts of the process to move together to support the next link in the process and to make it all work.

On a dairy farm, the goal is to produce milk, and that milk, in turn, is used to make other products, including the milk we drink, cheese, and, the most important, ice cream. To make all this work and the farm to keep running, people need to follow processes.

I'll explain with a short story about a dairy farm process. When you are a little guy, you can get hurt on the farm. Even when you grow up, the animals are big and heavy, and if they step on your feet, the result is broken bones or worse. In our little milk barn, the cows would be brought to a holding pen. This pen had concrete floors, and it was always spotlessly clean after every milking. But when the cows came in, it got filthy dirty. So, the first step in our process (keep in mind that this is now considered an old-school way of milking) was to bring the cows into the holding area. We opened a big, swinging gate that allowed entry to the milking area, and when closed, it worked as a fence to direct the cows out of the barn, down another path, and back out to the pasture and feeding areas. Seems simple enough, right?

To start the milking process, we would let in twelve cows (with twelve stanchions to put them in—again, old school). Once they had all placed themselves at or in the stanchion they chose (there is feed in place to make them put their head through the gate that holds them), we would lock them in (remember this; it's an important part of this story). After the initial twelve cows were in place, we would pull a steel wire above the entrance, and the stanchion would close, preventing the cow from backing out while milking. When we were done milking each cow, we opened her stanchion and she backed out, turning and heading down the path and back to the feeding area or pasture.

The barn had six milking machines and twelve cows, so we could only milk six at a time with the others in waiting. Then we would replace six cows at a time until we were done with the whole herd. This is the internal milking process—one small part of the overall process of raising cows on a dairy farm. We won't get into the processes related to growing, fixing, feeding, buying, and selling. All the moving parts that go into the entire process, including the person who drives the milk truck and delivers it to the creamery for processing, have to work together so we can enjoy the results.

Every day, I learned something amazing. Everyone in this process respected those who contributed to the overall success of the farm. The auction owner who sold the cattle never thought they were better than the person who picked up the milk, and the grain salesperson didn't look down on the farmer as just some guy or gal who milked cows. There was a common respect and an appreciation for each person's role in the process. This all worked because they understood each other's value and contribution to making it all happen.

WHEN THE COWS LIE DOWN

One fine fall day when I was a small kid, I was "helping" with the milking. I brought the cows up and opened the gate (you have to be able to count to twelve during this part), let the cows in, and watched as they promptly loaded into the stanchions. Then came the fun part. I had to slightly jump, grab the wire, and let my weight come down to lock all the cows in place—that is, if the wire didn't slip out of my hands. This is where I screwed up the process. Cows were milked twice a day, and when it was time, they were so ready that the holding area I described would have milk all over it from the leaking udders; the cows needed to be milked, badly!

As I was locking in the first twelve eager animals for their relief, the wire slipped from my hands. The latches to the stanchions half-closed and reopened with a loud bang. The cows, being creatures of habit, all backed out as if they were done for the day. I was all alone, standing between twelve cows heading out of the barn, intent on getting back to feed and pasture. This was a total mismatch, and the only thing I may have done right was to get the hell out of the way. Where could I head them off? How could I get them to turn back and stop twelve thousand pounds of animal heading out to feed?

Well, this one turned out okay, but only after a delay in the milking and me getting fired from that part of the process for the day. As they say, nobody got hurt, but I did have to clean up.

As I took these lessons with me to my time in the military and civilian leadership positions, I noticed that not all organizations had the same level of respect and admiration for all of those in their processes. Throughout my time working in hospitals and medical care, I went out of my way to thank cleaning staff, people preparing meals, and administrative support to remind them that it all starts and ends with them.

When I was in North Dakota, I had a fellow Chief Master Sergeant (the top enlisted rank in the Air Force) friend who lived near me, and we both spent time together while off duty. These types of relationships are invaluable when you are working on the Air Force issues that make the process of defending our nation work. That is a huge process that starts in many different places but ultimately has the goal of national security. On our base, we flew air refueling tankers to help our bombers and fighters stay flying while in combat and training. This requires a lot of maintenance, and my buddy was the Chief who made sure it happened on a daily basis.

This Chief was a great leader, as anointed by me and many more, and he was easy to work with. One day, he called me and wasn't his cheerful self as he asked what was going on in our medical group. He was upset and unhappy about our part of the process. The Chief proceeded to tell me that one of his maintainers had come for a medical appointment and had arrived a couple minutes late. My Airmen, in fine medic fashion, said, "You are late. You will need to reschedule." They paid no attention to his patch, his scent of jet fuel, and that he was hustling to get to the appointment and his clinic for care. My medics did it by the book, except they were missing a piece. They didn't have a full appreciation for the entire process and failed to recognize that it's more than just theirs.

While the maintainer was off the flightline at a medical appointment (which he now had to reschedule), the planes were not getting fixed. When the planes aren't fixed, they don't fly. The bombers and fighters then don't get their training time, and as you can see, the process breaks down. I was upset beyond imagination but knew I needed to get both sides of the story before reacting. So, off I went to the clinic to see what happened. When I asked the front desk people and the Airmen in charge, I heard just what I thought would be the case. "Chief, the policy says if you are late you have to reschedule, so we followed that process."

My response was this: "Have you ever seen what it takes for a maintainer to get on and off a flightline to do their work? Have you ever checked out a toolbox and gear required to work around the aircraft? Have you ever been to the flightline?" Their answer was a resounding "No." This was not their fault. They were not bad or malicious people; they just didn't understand the entire process they were a part of and how their actions could positively or negatively affect that.

I returned to my office, called the Chief back, and had him send his guy back to get him squared away. I thought about the farm, the process, and the respect and understanding by all involved. It made me quickly jump up and head to the commander's office. The Colonel was a good-hearted guy. He was open to the development and growth of the team, and I was hoping he would buy into my idea. I asked the Colonel for enough money to buy three sizes of cold-weather gear. He looked at me like I was crazy and asked, "Why?" As I relayed the story of the farm and then told him about the maintainer and the flightline, I said, "I am scheduling every one of our enlisted folks to go work on the flightline for a day. They need to see the process and feel their world to better take care of them."

The Colonel, to my surprise, said, "Send the officers too."

I was jumping for joy inside because this would be fun! I called my buddy the Chief and pitched the idea (this could only be done between the first of November and the last day of March—North Dakota is brutal then), and he quickly gave me the names of the people who would run that experiment. Off we went! First, we sent the Airmen who were involved in the initial issue. When they returned from doing fuel cell work (that part of maintenance is on a *Dirty Jobs* episode on TV), they were smiling ear to ear. They said things like, "We never knew about any of that stuff!" and "How cool are those planes?" and "It is great to be in the Air Force." The one thing I wanted to hear came right after that: "Chief, I get it. It takes forever to get off the flightline and to get over to our clinic."

Darn right it does. Mentoring, growth, and motivation all from a fuel cell. It was a win.

Roll forward to not long after that, and we did the same thing in Iraq. We had maintainers in the operating rooms assisting with combat casualties, and we had medics work on planes and ammo for combat missions. This carried over, and if you search YouTube, you'll find a short video of it in Iraq. Taking the time to do that was worth every minute and helped make our process and organization stronger as we built future leaders. I thank the Colonel and my Chief buddy Mike for making that happen!

LESSONS FROM MEDICS DOING MAINTENANCE

- To truly lead, you need to understand the entire system and process and your role in it—share that vision.
- The cows followed their process to a fault; if they knew the entire process, they wouldn't have run out of the barn.
- Taking time to explain the bigger picture is not a waste—do it and don't talk down to people when you share.
- Change your vantage point of how you see the world; it makes you a better and more informed leader and contributor.
- Feeling someone else's pain is good productive pain, and it makes you an advocate and better contributor—be brave and go do it.
- The Colonel didn't think his officers were above the task or too important to not participate—make sure those who may have cool positions get the opportunity of perspective. We are never too old, educated, or experienced to learn.

- One way of seeing things is just that—ONE way!
- Your aperture is yours to adjust—self-motivate and self-develop—put yourself out there and keep learning.
- Here are the URLs to access the video and article:
  - usafe.af.mil/News/Features/Display/Article/257458/flight-operators-go-to-the-operating-table-in-career-field-swap/
  - dvidshub.net/video/51762/medics-maintainers

Clear the Beds

At times, we experience events that seem unreal when we reflect on them, almost as if they never happened. Before I started to write the first word of this chapter, I called a dear friend and one of my leaders during a unique and trying time. I will call him Doc; he was also the leader who carried a tremendous burden as we made decisions of incredible magnitude. With his permission and collaboration, this chapter will be ours to share from a joint perspective.

Doc and I worked through clearing the beds and preparing for what would be a major operation during the surge in Iraq.

Clearing the beds means to empty an entire hospital ahead of a major military offensive. It is prepping for mass casualties. Those of us who are critical of our leaders and think we could do it better can more deeply appreciate those who take on such decisions and responsibilities. We can better realize how lonely it can be for the one who has to make the call and then execute it.

When I was growing up in a rural community, I was exposed to leaders in less traditional ways. My examples of leaders included farmers (of course), business owners, a baseball coach or two, cops, firefighters, and all the elected officials around. As I watched the farmers conduct their business and daily operations, they made decisions constantly: *Do I send the cow to slaughter? Do I plant or not plant? Do I sell or buy?* They also decide what they can and can't do; vacations are but a dream, and supporting their kids and their growth drives priorities. It amazed me how natural it seemed. These men and women would just start by putting the decision into motion and then managing and leading it. Sometimes it didn't go well, but mostly it seemed *easy*. It wasn't until I started to lead people and manage resources with high value that I understood what goes on in the leader's mind—the lost sleep, the seeking counsel and advice, and the reading and research that go with preparation. It takes constant work to be the most informed and capable leader you can be before you make big decisions, and all the while, you manage the dynamics that go along with change.

When my grandfather decided to move his entire farming operation from the California northern coast to the northern valley, I am sure he had many conversations and sleepless nights. There were kids to consider (my mother would move in the middle of high school), and he had to ask advice from my grandmother. In the end, when it came time to decide, it was his decision, and all that comes with it weighed on him.

When asked how he felt about making the decision to invade Normandy in June of 1944, General Eisenhower said that the best night's sleep he got was after he made the decision to go, for at that moment, it was up to others to execute the mission. I am sure he worried, and he definitely led and managed through the end of the war and beyond. But in this case, his weight of command was immense in that he had lots of advice, data, and history to work with. It is a lonely existence when you consider all that, and the whole world is looking at you to make the call, set the direction, and move out. Once you start things like that in motion, there is no going back. When we were told to clear the beds in 2008, it was not done in haste, and it was not done without heartfelt and deep thought.

In the spring of 2008, we had many operations going on during the surge that brought unique influxes to our trauma center; at times we experienced deeply tragic moments. One dynamic that had started to rise was that the enemy was continually harassing part of Baghdad with rockets and mortars. This attack would require significant operations to neutralize and ultimately eliminate the threat. This was one of those decisions that I alluded to earlier, and I am sure it was not taken lightly, as it meant that we would have significant casualties to achieve the mission. This event started the domino effect that would come into our medical world and into our military responsibilities to execute our portion of the mission. This would soon become a deeply dividing emotional event between leaders of a medical unit filled with people who were torn between the responsibilities that come with both. In this case, the core values that drive each of these professions would collide and drive human emotions in a way I had never experienced before or since.

To set the stage for those who are not steeped in military doctrine and operations, there is a whole process to how you fight and go to war. It is not as simple as taking some tanks over there, and taking that ground or getting the enemy—it is very complex and requires extreme logistics, planning, resource massing, and just-in-time training. Each operation is unique and requires collaboration between the services involved. All of this has to be ready to go before the "tanks" are sent forward. In these situations, the medical piece is also complex. For example, recent intelligence reports that before the Russians invaded Ukraine, a key indicator of the imminent invasion was the fact that the medical units had started to bring blood supplies to the frontlines. This is one of those building blocks that must be in place before you send in the tanks. In our case, as we prepared to eliminate this threat, we knew there would be multiple casualties over a course of many days. So, we received the order to "Clear the beds!"

Clear the beds sounds like a hard and painful event and a lot of work. In reality, in most non-combat hospitals, this is easier than it sounds. The challenge is regarding the critical care beds for extremely ill people. Our situation was odd and complex. There are often emotions attached to any patient we care for, especially with the amount of skill and expertise required to keep these people alive as we try to send them home to their loved ones. There were three categories of patients in the hospital at the time: Allies (Americans or other allies, including civilian personnel), Iraqis (those who are indigenous to the country—men, women, and children—and non-combatants), and the enemy (yes, we took care of the enemy right alongside the rest).

In our hospital, the American wounded were evacuated in twenty-four to forty-eight hours, no matter how badly hurt they were. This was an amazing feat performed daily by incredible people; we got the patients home to more definitive care that was closer to their loved ones. If patients were allied members, it was fast but maybe not as fast; still, we got you home, too. For the indigenous patients who were severely injured and required intensive care, our hospital was almost always the best place to be. Here they had the best chance of survival and rehabilitation. So often, we had many intensive care beds full of indigenous patients—yes, including the enemy. These patients (these people, rather) became part of our lives, as did the assigned Soldiers, Sailors, Airmen, and Marines who guarded the enemy patients 24/7. It was common to look down the bay of patients and see three or four guards sitting at the bedside. We did it all.

The healthcare in Iraq at this time was fractured, and most civilian facilities didn't have the capabilities we had. It was always dropping them down a level or two in care when we moved them. The goal was to get them as healthy as possible before we moved them, and they mainly went to the hospitals in Baghdad. This happened frequently—usually one or two at a time—and our docs took them on the helicopters to Baghdad.

We had dedicated and highly passionate professional people who were charged with these transfers. We were all passionate about our patients, no matter who they were. I watched, on more than one occasion, as an enemy patient would throw urine or feces at our Airmen. I helped clean up a few times after these events, and yet after all that, our caregivers continued to care for each of them like they were the most important persons in the room. I bet you have a bit of emotion and many questions right now. Multiply them by hundreds, and you can get to the place where I am going to take you.

The beds were cleared for a few reasons. One was because an allied member needed a bed, so room was made, usually through transfer. We also cleared the beds in the case of a mass casualty event, and we cleared the beds when military planning and doctrine dictated that the beds would be empty prior to a major operation where many casualties were expected. Once this order was placed, it was on the hospital command staff to execute it. The person who held the full responsibility was the commander—the leader of the whole smash. Remember, this book is about *quitting* or not quitting, so I will tell you now that the actions of the leader and the navigation he had to make in what I am about to describe were no less than amazing. I don't know more than a handful of commanders in my time who would have maintained their temper, grace, and respect any better.

So, yes, we had civilians in our hospital and intensive units; some had been there for months and had undergone multiple surgeries. We knew their names, and some even had family members come to visit. They were there so long—an odd dynamic in the middle of a war, right? Yes, we also had the enemy. No visitors, but surely there for a long while and well known to us. And we always had our own, getting ready to be moved to Germany and then home. We were usually full. When the order came to clear the beds, we had enough going on in the hospital that we needed to make difficult decisions quickly and execute them with precision and expertise.

We had the right people for all of this, but what we hadn't anticipated was the added dimension of knowing what may come of the patients we had to "clear." We knew the practices of the Iraqi medical systems; they were not like our own. In this case, they did not have the resources to sustain these patients. There was a high probability that after all these months of care, these people would not survive. In the eyes of some of our team, they were convinced that this was true, and, worse yet, they felt that if they participated in the clearing of the beds, then they were essentially "killing them." Things were said like, "I will not participate in euthanasia." The emotions ran hot, and quickly there became two camps.

Remember, I told you, this needed to be planned and executed quickly; there wasn't time to vote or develop elaborate alternatives. We were going to do the normal transfer process, just in mass and volume, and quickly. All hands on deck, as it were. Well, we had a problem. Many of the key people in that process felt that the oath they took was of the highest calling in this situation. Higher than their officership, their command position, or the direct military orders given to them. They did not want to participate, and they were highly emotional about it—they were in the decision stages of "do I or don't I *quit*."

This was a powerful moment, under direct orders, while in a combat zone, and the ramifications of disobeying could be up to execution (no, we don't do that anymore, but it is still on the books). You can face extreme discipline and stand to lose an awful lot in the end. Here we were in a swirl of emotions around patients we knew, a process that was not desirable, morals, values, credos, and medical professional beliefs. All of it was colliding.

This is when you are defined as a leader; these are the moments when you are all alone (see a similar story in *Make the Tough Call* in my first book).

My deepest personal memory of this as the Chief was interacting with my fellow Airmen and medical professionals who were absolutely against it. I had my orders; the boss was clear, and now we needed to move out and clear the beds. We knew the potential outcomes, and we knew who might be filling that bed in the next twenty-four to forty-eight hours: our men and women who were headed to the fight. As I spoke to the staff—some new to the Air Force and others who had been around for a long time—and listened to their concerns, I had mixed emotions. I am a Registered Nurse, and I had a calling and an oath. But I am also an American Airman, and I had my orders. It was a double dilemma, for sure. I felt these individuals' passion and their desire to honor both the oath and the order and make it all better. The fact was we had to pick the best of a few bad choices and then commit to it, and execute or *quit*. This is where leaders show their true colors, and how they shape the decision and execute it matters forever.

I would like to say that everyone came around to the belief that clearing the beds was okay because our fighters were going in them and because our orders were our orders and disobeying was treasonous. I wish that were the case. We had congressional inquiries that lasted long after we all rotated back to the world, and we had anger. Frankly, we lost a few people in the areas of enthusiasm or commitment. Those losses were few, though, because the leader did his magic. He listened, he heard, he explained why (both his reasons and the mission), he gave clear expectations and desired outcomes, he ensured we had what we needed to make it happen, he had our backs and our fronts when the exterior forces played into all this, and most of all, he *cared* about all of us. No matter what side of the issue we fell on, he respected our beliefs and wanted us all to have some foundation after it was over to stay, not *quit*, and be ready for the next mission. There is always a next mission, a next tough decision, and a next order that sounds like "clear the beds" that we will need to be ready for.

Did we clear the beds? Yes, with military precision. Did we like the results that occurred for our indigenous patients? Of course not; all of us wished we had a better bad option. Did we quit? Maybe some quit on the Air Force that day; maybe some dumped the good attitude and commitment. But I didn't see anybody *quit*, because the real reason to do that is more about how the leader handles it versus the actual issue at hand. We cleared the beds, we did it well, and we met the mission. The difficult part of all of this, however, was that the major operation that drove this directive was canceled. We never received a mass casualty, and we never got any of our patients back. There was no way to predict that situation and no way we could have taken the risk. The leadership challenge that goes with this part of the story requires a daily commitment to the ideals I mentioned—we were led in a way that didn't produce *quitters*. It created future leaders, showed us an example to follow as we continued on, and definitely showed us how to make tough calls.

LESSONS FROM CLEAR THE BEDS

- Respect toward those who disagree with your direction sometimes grows new followers.
- Listening to all viewpoints can steady the emotions and calm the seas.
- Setting the direction and providing clarity are life skills in every avenue we operate in—your team and, better yet, your family will love you for it.

- If it is your call to make, gather data and then make the call. If you hesitate, you may lose your teammates and your command.
- The best decision is sometimes the best of a few really bad options—be okay with that and know that it is not going to magically change.
- Teams succeed and fail on the back of the leader—build a tough team before a crisis.
- Have your people's backs and fronts—they need to be able to focus. This includes your kids and spouse or significant other.

Don't Lead by Hitting the Send Button

Why in the world would you lose good people, watch them disengage, or allow them to "quiet quit" because of your emails or text messages?

Because of my age, I saw the transition from a paper-and-pen-driven world to one driven by technology. It was a transition to diminishing leadership development and leadership skills, in my opinion. In my early days, I developed a lot of soft skills as a leader by writing down my notes and delivering them in person as direction, feedback, and orders.

This was just the way we had to do it. We would never have a critical conversation with our people or a group if it wasn't communicated in person. Then came the computer and interconnection. The wonderful world of being able to connect anywhere around the globe and at all times of the day. What a lifesaver, right? No more walking the form, notes, or directives down the hall to somebody's office; now we could just hit the send button.

You picked up this book for a reason, and this may well be your favorite chapter because when we are curious as to the cause of why things happen that affect us negatively, we tend to want to hear from people who have been there and done that. Some of us have certainly learned a few lessons from hitting the send button, or not.

When I speak to groups or lead a disaster management team, I tell them, "There are two types of communications. Too much, or not enough." Herein lies the struggle between communication and leadership. Is it true if you are the leader that once you hit the send button with that perfectly crafted four- or five-paragraph email that your charges will read every line, interpret it exactly as you meant, and be 100 percent on board from the minute they read it? NO! So, should you send the email at all, or is there a balance?

Expediency saves money, cuts personnel costs, and lets us do more work in the finite amount of time we have in a day, week, or year. It also is the death knell of leadership.

So why are people quiet quitting? I argue that it is partially because there is a speed limit of leadership that leaves no time for the human element—the walk down the hall to have a face-to-face conversation—and leaves an opening for an excuse during a time of failure that sounds much like this: "I put that in the email." Really?! In which of the 1,500 words?

As most people progress through the ranks of leadership, they are not interested in repeating what they have already done; they are ready for the next challenge and learning. This is where they forget where they came from. They try to lead under the assumption that people doing the job they used to do have the same challenges, receive the same direction, and are guided by the same vision as themselves, and if they just write their concerns, needs, and directions in an email, then it will be consumed in the same fashion. This is false. When people are walking out your door or talking about you in a way that is not flattering, it usually stems from the levels of assumptions and ambiguity you have demonstrated and developed that make them go find a place without those qualities.

I once received some direct and harsh feedback on the number of emails I was sending. Most of it was forwarded messages I wanted to share and information I believed to be important, but nonetheless, it was, to the leaders below me, clutter; I wasn't respecting their time. It was a dilemma for me because I would also get feedback about sharing what I knew. To solve this problem, I left the office and followed up the email with a visit. I changed the speed limit a bit to allow for clarification, and the two forms of communication seemed to work well (most of the time, anyway).

Let me leave you with this: What if I wrote you an email today that said we all need to exercise more, so you must be at the walking park every morning for exercise. But when you show up, I'm not there? What would you do? What decisions would you make about your future? How would you feel about the leader? The answers to those questions are the answer to the question: why are people leaving or "*quitting*?" We can find some simple lessons to abide by.

LESSONS FROM THE SEND BUTTON

- Your personality and intent are never truly understood in an email.
- Expediency is a powerful thing, so use it wisely and don't get intoxicated with it.
- Your intent and direction are best conveyed in person—use the right communication vehicle.
- Don't do hard work with an email; you lose respect. Hard conversations need to take place face to face.
- Once sent, emails don't come back.

Leadership Starts with the Leader— Why Do Your People Leave You, the BOSS?

We all have a story of failure or something we wish we had done better on our leadership journeys—whether in our household or in our work. We sometimes dwell on these failures and tell the stories over and over as examples of how we made a wrong move. It is much more uncommon to talk about the successes, the change we made, the triumph in our world, or whatever positivity it may be.

Leaders, today I woke up feeling clear-headed, sober, and sharp-minded as I went for decaf coffee. I was reflecting on how leaders quietly project themselves on their people, their followers, and their personal inner circle. They project praise for good work and opportunities to improve. If you haven't heard of it, look up Johari's window to get an understanding of what you don't know about yourself, but others know about you. Remember, you know details about others that they don't. Visit this website to learn more: communicationtheory.org/the-johari-window-model.

So why am I talking about Johari's window and waking up sober, and how does this relate to why your people may be leaving you? Today I am celebrating a success, not a failure. On June 3, 2018, I took my last drink—it was the absolute best decision I ever made. That decision was reinforced by how my day started today. This is not going to be a story about me; if you want the whole story about my breakup and divorce with alcohol, you can get it all in my first book.

Your people see you every day (or not—more on that in a minute), so they know your norms better than you do. They know when you are off, they know what pushes your buttons, and they know when you have a hangover. They know your HABITS! Once they have your habits memorized, they start to give themselves permission to act like you, conduct themselves like you, and forgive themselves for less-than-upstanding performance because you "do the same thing." If you don't believe me, ask or watch your kids or other kids. So, why do your people leave? I'll relay what I hear as I mentor, coach, and speak on these issues.

Your people are leaving for a few basic reasons. These reasons often include the fact that they never see you, you say one thing and do another, or you have favorites (even though you think it doesn't show). Also, they may feel disenfranchised or, worse, disrespected. Ultimately, perhaps you don't treat them respectfully. It amazes me that a clinic or hospital will hire a doctor to focus on one area like infectious disease, have him dedicate a decade of his life to his work, and then tell him during COVID that the executive team has a better approach to the pandemic. This isn't a hypothetical situation; a real doctor quit the institution and entirely quit the profession. This story is not unique, either. I know ICU nurses who now sell cars as they quit their boss and their profession because of their leaders and the example they set. I get asked over and over again, "Why am I losing good people who have been here forever ... and can you help?"

When I go into an organization that is facing these issues, the first thing I do is ask a few questions. These questions always start at the top. I ask, "If you think the ship is sinking, have you gone below deck to look at the leak, or are you rearranging the deck chairs?" In a real-life scenario, this looks like a rebranding, a new set of values (usually not lived up to), or a new strategic plan. Your people couldn't care less, especially the good ones.

What you need is a strategic plan of presence, respect, and showing that you walk the walk. You are not scared to help keep the ship afloat from the bowels of the organization—it is called courage and leading by example. Check your Johari's window, go put on some jeans, and work with the grounds maintenance people for a day or talk to a cook in the cafeteria. What you'll find out is the answer to the question as to why people are leaving YOU! That is when the work starts! People knew I drank. I was lucky enough to get where I got. My greatest accomplishment has been changing my strategic plan and rebranding ME!

LESSONS FROM LEADERSHIP STARTS WITH THE LEADER

- If you feel disorganized, look at your plan. Odds are it doesn't exist.
- When you lead or fly with the eagles, someone is always watching, and some will want to shoot you down.
- The mirror you use as a leader is always a two-way mirror: who is on the other side and what do they see?
- When you show people who you are, they will believe you.

Quit Lowering the Bar

I have been asked, on occasion, to give my impression of an organization based on the fact that their team—or their product—has not hit the proverbial home run they want. Their competition is gaining on or passing them, and the margins are shrinking. They want to know what magic pill they can take to fix it. When I prescribe the elixir to them and describe how to take this magic potion, many of them make a face and say things like, "I don't think we can do that here!" or better yet, "That is not possible." It saddens me because the elixir tastes just fine, and if taken and used as prescribed, it would make them stronger, more competitive, and more productive.

I write about slowing down to go faster, and my points involve avoiding mistakes that cause repeat work or accidents that can damage an organization, but my point here is not about slowing down. It is about doing the hard things while maintaining a culture and standard that is acceptable and, frankly, is not compromised for any reason. If a compromise occurs, the consequence should be exclusion from the group. That sounds harsh, but you are reading this book because you want to know why people *quit*. And maybe you are reading this book because you have a problem to solve.

On the farm, we had super high standards; I don't think this is widespread knowledge. I remember as a young boy when the milk truck would pull into the yard; I heard the tires crunching the gravel and saw the big, silver, shiny tank sparkling in the sun. Usually, it was the same milk truck driver every time. It was a part of an entire routine that is pretty neat. You see, you get to sell the milk, and with that comes a check. With that check comes the bill paying, and so on down the line. I love to watch this process: the truck would back up to the tank shed—this shed was the cleanest place on the farm, and for good reason. The tank was always so cold, and the pumps made a specific whirring sound as the big paddles kept the milk stirred so it wouldn't separate. This all went on until the milk truck showed up.

The driver would jump from the truck and have the usual little bullshit session with us. Then he would take all the items off the truck as necessary to pull the milk from the tank to the truck, leaving us with an empty tank to clean and eventually fill back up. That sounds like an easy task, right? Actually, it is not, and it is very detailed. The process starts with the driver taking a small, stainless-steel ladle, which looks like a shot glass on a stick, and dipping it in the tank to collect a shot of milk (actually, a few of these). This milk was placed in glass containers, labeled with the farm name, and set aside to be processed at the lab. This was done for a number of reasons, and it was all about standards. Those samples were tested for everything from butter fat content to levels of bacteria in the milk (yes, all milk has bacteria, but is it too dirty?). If you don't meet the standards, you could be penalized or, worse, the whole batch could be discarded and you don't get paid. This is why we always cleaned the cows before the machines are placed to milk them, and we made a big deal of it. Imagine if you took that shortcut, and what would end up happening? It had consequences all down the line, including making someone sick. These same concepts apply to raising meat animals and crop management. Farms are places of high standards.

I know farmers who lowered their standards as they sought to achieve lower costs, quicker completion times, or less use of resources, basically to pinch pennies and save money. The outcomes of this were never good, and at times resulted in people getting hurt.

So, let's get off the farm and back to whatever world you are in. Does this play into why people *quit* YOU? I watched a movie on a flight recently. Everyone had been going nuts over it, and it was a tear-jerker for some. Most mentioned coming away with some national pride and feeling pretty good about things. I had almost all those thoughts, and being a thirty-year military man, it moved me. But I also saw a part in the movie that made me cringe, as I realized it demonstrated why people leave organizations and leaders.

This movie was *Top Gun: Maverick*. It is action-packed and entertaining, it mixes the old with the new, and it outlines a new challenge that our men and women in uniform face while protecting our interests and our freedoms. During the movie, the team training for this nearly impossible mission had a mishap. The accident was caused by learning and growing into the necessary parameters needed to be successful; they had set standards and necessary goals to make the mission work. Then mistakes were made.

First, the most qualified person (the subject-matter expert) was removed; next, the boss who removed him took over; and finally, he changed the standards for the team by lowering the bar to make it easier and more achievable. He basically started a process of milking dirty cows. Now, luckily, it got corrected in short order (go see the movie for all the details), but what if it hadn't been corrected? What if the new standards had become THE standards? The boss would say, "I eliminated all potential for error, everyone passed the test (100 percent is good—right?), and look at how good we are," right up until they flew the mission, got shot down, and the mission failed.

"The mission failed." Think about that. Consider that mission success requires COURAGE. Followers love courage, they love integrity (a form of moral courage), and they respect standards and accountability. When these qualities fail, the standards are lowered and inconsistently enforced. People feel unsure, unappreciated, and, worst of all, disrespected. So, ask yourself, "How much effort toward excellence are they putting in? How much attention to detail are they applying, and how are they treating the customers and the product?" If your bottom line is suffering and you are losing what you call the "good" people, but you can't put your finger on the reason, then ask yourself, "Is my organization full of courage, or full of something else?"

Moving the bar up is helpful when you are growing people or businesses and you are making your team stronger. Where you spend your time on people matters; do you reward and develop the teammates who have high standards and are high performing so you retain and promote a culture of "staying"? Or do the less motivated get all your attention, and do you lower everyone's bar so they can play on an even field of mediocrity? Moving the bar down is usually the reaction to a tough problem. It's an easy way to get the "numbers" or to complete the job. You have seen it before; it sounds like this: "Why did that bridge fail and kill all those people?" or "What do you mean medical students cheated on tests?" "The reason I got sick was because somebody didn't wash a cow, test the milk, or pasteurize it properly because they lowered a standard."

People (especially good ones) want to be a part of something great. They know what great looks like to them, and they will stay for a long time just to be a part of it. Most people also know when they and their team are compromised or misled based on motivations driven by money or self-promotion. These motivations usually cause poor decisions. Listen to a few exit interviews if you can.

LESSONS FROM THE LOWERED BAR

- The standard you so want to deviate from is there for a reason—do your homework before you violate it and hurt somebody.
- People who see a lack of courage from their leaders will find a new leader.
- Weakness and compromise breed weakness and compromise.
- A lack of integrity and accountability is a culture—you own that.
- Do the hard things and maintain the standards—it grows people and the bottom line.
- What is your reputation? Find out because you have earned it.
- People don't *quit* championship teams; they actually take less money to stay.
- Respect—do you show it? If not, you can expect *quitting*.

Navigating PTSD and Moral Injury

Within the shadows of trauma, two steadfast companions loom: post-traumatic stress disorder (PTSD) and moral injury. As the owner of both, I have forged an intimate relationship with these silent warriors that accompany me daily. They simultaneously remind me how easy it is to quit and how rewarding it is to follow my intention and determination to not quit.

Moral injury embodies the psychological and spiritual anguish that ensues when one witnesses or engages in actions that transgress their deeply ingrained moral beliefs and values. While often associated with high-stress professions like the military, healthcare, and first responders, moral injury can manifest in any context where individuals confront morally challenging situations.

The weight of moral injury has shaped my existence in profound ways. As a military veteran, I found myself caught in a web of moral dilemmas, forced to make excruciating decisions that violated my core principles. The toll it took on my soul was immeasurable, plunging me into a sea of guilt and shame and a sense of betrayal. In accepting these experiences, I have sought to harness their transformative energy, using my stories and emotions as a catalyst for helping to heal others and enlightening those in helping roles who may not have experienced similar traumas.

The world has a dire need for understanding. When I received three phone calls in a single day from friends and family scattered across the nation, all seeking clarity on moral injury, it ignited the realization that many others are also grappling with this concept. Moral injury, distinct from PTSD, delves into the inner conflict that arises from violating one's moral compass. It elicits emotions such as guilt, shame, and a shattered trust in oneself and others. Unlike PTSD, it does not solely stem from combat or traumatic experiences but can emerge from a variety of contexts.

The prevalence of PTSD and moral injury among veterans in the United States is alarmingly high. Both conditions need multifaceted support and assistance to create healing. Veterans' stories, often left untold, hold the key to unlocking empathy and understanding.

Beyond a fleeting "Thank you for your service" lies a world of untold narratives. Engaging veterans in conversation, inviting them to share their stories, unlocks profound connections and bridges understanding. We all face complexities and challenges, and we all can set an intention and determination not to quit. Together, let us march onward, offering support, compassion, and a listening ear to those whose journeys have been shaped by PTSD and moral injury. Onward!

LESSONS FROM PTSD AND MORAL INJURY

- Everything in life drives energy, and what you do with it is yours to control. Turn it into positive energy.
- Take the walk into the scary place, engage, find out, and grow.
- Build everlasting bridges; you'll need them. Don't burn them because of spite or anger.

Overcoming Pain and Fear

I recently watched another movie on a long plane flight. Anyone who has been on a twelve-hour (or longer) plane flight knows the routine—eat, sleep, and watch movies. I also find long flights to be great opportunities to think. In the movie, one of the main characters was dying and had a lot of unfinished business with important people in his life. The problem was, however, that he had suffered a massive stroke and was no longer conscious.

As his family gathered around him, they asked if there was an opportunity for him to regain his awareness and maybe have an opportunity to discuss these loose ends. The elder in the scene said, "He is the sum of his days. He will not write his story any further." This simple quip got me thinking: "Why do people have these moments when loose ends are left unaddressed? Why haven't they gone and done—or at least tried—things they may have dreamed of? Why do they leave the wide-open holes, thinking that someday they may sort it out, and then it is too late!"

The two barriers that keep us from being who we want to be and getting where we want to go are pain and fear. The multitude of reasons we make the excuse to not try something or not say or do the things we dream about boil down to pain and fear. It's precisely why we sometimes quit activities or efforts that we truly want to do or accomplish. These are the "what-ifs" in life that paralyze us and make us less effective as leaders and people.

In this book, we have considered many lessons about quitting—both good and bad—and what drives us to want to quit. Is it as simple as a choice, or is it driven by two real barriers of pain and fear that we need to confront to get us to the point where we can realize our dreams and become who we want to be and go where we want to go?

As I reflect on agriculture and the people who choose that lifestyle, the traits that stick out are persistence, self-belief, and staying focused on the goal. There are a hundred reasons to quit on a farm. They include not enough money, not enough time, and the rate and physicality of the work. No matter how you look at it, it is daunting and requires dealing with the natural pain and fear that are ever-present in our lives.

When it comes to what influences us, think about what we consume and how we consume it. Would a news station make much money if the stories were all happy and ended happy? No way! What interests us the most are topics that are scary, painful, and difficult. As long as it is someone else involved, we find it grotesquely entertaining. But what it also does is drive fear and show pain; it makes us tell ourselves, "I am glad that is not me" or "I could never go through what they did." Why do we choose to draw negative outcomes with our self-talk, and why do we often see the barriers in situations and relationships? Instead, we can visualize positive outcomes and see ourselves crossing the finish line first.

I play golf—poorly, but I play. One reason I play is to calm my mind and keep me focused on the task. The planning and the strategy it takes to make a shot, set up for the next shot, and so on allow me to focus. I usually play my best when my mood is cheerful, as I feel good and the company with me is enjoyable. I also play better when I visualize a shot: where it is going to fly, where it will land, and the positives of a well-struck ball. I also notice when my thoughts of "Don't go in the water" or "Don't hit it left" creep in, and it usually ends up not turning out so well.

As I was watching a golf event on TV, the number one player in the world started the final round four strokes behind the field. By the twelfth hole, he had caught up and had an eight-foot putt to take the lead. The play-by-play announcer was the best in the business, and both of his color commentators were Hall of Fame major champions. As the world's number one was sizing up his putt, the announcer asked the two Hall of Famers what they thought he would do with the putt. Most of us were waiting to hear their ideas on how hard to hit it or the break in the putt. It floored me when both of them, almost simultaneously, said words like "He is going to ram it in the back of the cup, take the lead, step on the rest of the field, and go on to victory."

They didn't know what would happen, they couldn't predict it, and what they were saying is what they had conditioned themselves to say their whole lives and throughout successful careers. It was positive self-talk, seeing nothing but good outcomes, and visualizing the end state in a victorious way. The world's number one missed the putt, and the next comment was that he had six more opportunities. They moved on while still staying positive. Can you imagine a farmer who always saw a hailstorm or a flood? Or a leader who always saw the team losing on the last play of the game? So why are fear and pain so powerful, and why are we geared to naturally see the missed putt or the lost crop? Is it how we educate ourselves? Is it who we surround ourselves with? Or is it what we *consume* that puts us at an immediate disadvantage to be who we want to be and get where we want to go?

How does this all reflect when we ask the question about why people *quit*? Sometimes, when we talk to ourselves in a way that builds and climbs the insurmountable wall, we tend to find the easiest way to address whatever the painful or scary thing is; a lot of times, quitting is easiest. So, if you are reading this with an open mind, I ask, "What kind of leader do you want to be? Is it integral, approachable, liked, or maybe even loved?"

Apply that same question to your relationships—what kind of mom, partner, dad, or friend do you want to be, and where do you want to go with it? The hurdle that you must overcome is to learn to visualize what you want. It is absolutely necessary for you to use self-talk in a way that motivates you and drives you to the place where you want to go. You must demonstrate it consistently and in a way that gets you to your goal. It is the eight-foot putt that you must make over and over again; it is the planting, the growing, and the harvest. It is consistency and repetitive positive actions that drive away the pain and the fear. I have never been in an academic environment where, if someone had put in the work, studied hard, and prepared properly, they were not only calm about taking a test, but they anticipated taking the test. Preparation is an elixir to both fear and pain.

I once read an unattributed quote said that says, "When respect stops being served, it is time to leave the table." That sounded like quitting to me when I first read it; however, as we look at situations that lack respect in our lives, both personal and professional, don't we find that the people who are unprepared and who self-talk in a negative way tend to be less respectful? Preparation includes respect for yourself and respecting those you lead.

There are a few constants in our lives that drive our mental approaches to all that we do. Some of these are in the form of trauma and moral injury. These self-talk attributes are key to surviving these conditions that shape us and are a part of us forever. So, to my fellow owners of PTSD and trauma, no matter how you got there, be kind to yourself, respect yourself, don't quit on yourself, and close the gap on finding positive people who can help you be the best you can be every day.

LESSONS FROM PAIN AND FEAR

- Be kind to yourself—you are your number one fan.
- What you consume becomes you, so watch what your diet when it comes to relationships, media, books, and entertainment..
- Always see yourself making the putt.
- Demand respect, but it starts with self-respect.
- Don't be the sum of your days when it is too late.
- Tell yourself how GREAT you are, because you are!
- Don't let a missed putt keep you from moving on to another opportunity.

Acknowledgments

To Kim and Paul, you touched my life forever, and I am blessed in that way forever. I still miss you, my friend.

To my "hero" and commander in Iraq, out of respect, I'll leave out your name. You are a true national treasure and a friend. Thank you, sir, for keeping me Max Fab and showing me the cows when I need help.

To my wife, Pat, who deserves a whole book just about her. Thank you for your belief in me, your love, and being my wingman and battlebuddy. You are the BEST!

Lastly, to all those people I mention in this book who shaped me in what to do and what NOT to do. Your lessons are invaluable and life-long.

About the Author

From a foundation built on growing up in an agricultural environment, Dave Nordel takes a lifetime of extraordinary experiences and demonstrates the power of "Giving Back." Grounded in both good and bad and thirty-plus years in the military, Dave harnesses the ability to lead at an executive level and to affect the lives of our nation's sons and daughters, both in peacetime and during conflict.

With forty years of military and civilian leadership, coaching, and mentoring, Dave has transitioned into sharing the gifts he has acquired in the hopes of building better leaders, better parents, and better people to close the gaps in our culture. He inspires all of us to improve ourselves through self-development and practicing good mental health.

Dave is a master storyteller and loves to give back through teaching at the collegiate level and in small groups. With a passion for veterans, Dave represents the veteran community with a focus on mental health, PTSD, moral injury, and suicide prevention. He founded Max Fab Consulting with the intention of sharing his talent of writing and speaking and his hope to make a difference for people who struggle with the traumas they carry.

An outdoorsman who loves all life has to offer, Dave finds his balance doing activities he is passionate about. He is a board member of Horse Spirits Healing, a nonprofit focused on equine therapy to assist veterans and their families with mental and physical health recovery and recuperation.

Dave is the proud father of two boys, Dominic and David, and has been married to Patricia for over thirty years. He is generous with his time, and he mentors aspiring adults to help them achieve their life and career goals. To share the gifts of Dave's experiences and life lessons, visit MaxFabConsulting.com.

www.ingramcontent.com/pod-product-compliance
Lightning Source LLC
Chambersburg PA
CBHW032051150426
43194CB00006B/495